Arizona's
Sanctuaries,
Retreats,
and
Sacred Places

Kelly Ettenborough

2003

Text and photography by
Kelly Ettenborough

WESTCLIFFE PUBLISHERS

www.westcliffepublishers.com

International Standard Book Number: 1-56579-438-9

Text and photography copyright: Kelly Ettenborough, 2003. All rights reserved.

Editor: Jenna Samelson Browning
Design Concept: Angie Lee, Grindstone Graphics
Production: Carol Pando and Craig Keyzer

Published by:
Westcliffe Publishers, Inc.
P.O. Box 1261
Englewood, CO 80150
www.westcliffepublishers.com

Printed in China through: H & Y Printing, Ltd.

Library of Congress Cataloging-in-Publication Data:

Ettenborough, Kelly.
    Arizona's sanctuaries, retreats, and sacred places / by Kelly Ettenborough.
        p. cm.
    Includes index.
    ISBN 1-56579-438-9 (pbk.)
        1. Religious institutions--Arizona--Guidebooks. 2. Sacred
    space--Arizona--Guidebooks. 3. Arizona--Guidebooks. I. Title.

BL2527.A6 .E88 2002
291.3'5'09791--dc21   2002029629

*For more information about other fine books and calendars from Westcliffe Publishers, please contact your local bookstore, call us at 1-800-523-3692, write for our free color catalog, or visit us on the Web at **www.westcliffepublishers.com**.*

Please Note: Risk is always a factor in backcountry and high-mountain travel. Many of the activities described in this book can be dangerous, especially when weather is adverse or unpredictable, and when unforeseen events or conditions create a hazardous situation. The author has done her best to provide the reader with accurate information about backcountry travel, as well as to point out some of its potential hazards. It is the responsibility of the users of this guide to learn the necessary skills for safe backcountry travel, and to exercise caution in potentially hazardous areas. The author and publisher disclaim any liability for injury or other damage caused by backcountry traveling or performing any other activity described in this book.

Cover Photo: Chapel of the Holy Cross, Sedona

Opposite: A painted image of Jesus on the cross at Mission in the Sun, Tucson

Acknowledgments

I always told my husband that I would dedicate my first book to him. I married my high school sweetheart, Trevor Ettenborough, in 1988. He's the best friend and personal computer tech-support expert anyone could want. Without his patience, map-reading skills, and ability to bring home take-out dinner, this book would not have been possible. Thanks for the compass.

Ivy at San José de Tumacácori Mission Church

We have a daughter, Ivy, a bright, 5-year-old bundle of energy who makes us proud to be her favorite people. She came with me on many excursions, pen and paper in hand "to take notes." Eventually, she will be able to read and will notice if I do not mention her name. She is likely to consider this a shortcoming on her mother's part.

I also want to thank Rose Tring, my editor at *The Arizona Republic*, for her support and patience as I completed this book; my fellow newspaper team members who gave me great ideas and cheered me on; my Monday night friends; and the rest of my family, in particular my mother, who took Ivy on "vacation" while I finished the book, and my sister, who said she understood why I forgot to send her a birthday present last January. Happy birthday, Megan.

Finally, I'd like to express my appreciation to Westcliffe Publishers— Linda Doyle especially, for the phone call that came one afternoon with this terrific opportunity, and Jenna Browning for her encouragement and kindness.

Opposite: Casa Malpais Archaeological Park

4

Contents

Regions of Arizona

Opposite: Mission in the Sun, Tucson

Regions of Arizona

Petroglyphs at V Bar V Ranch Heritage Site, Sedona

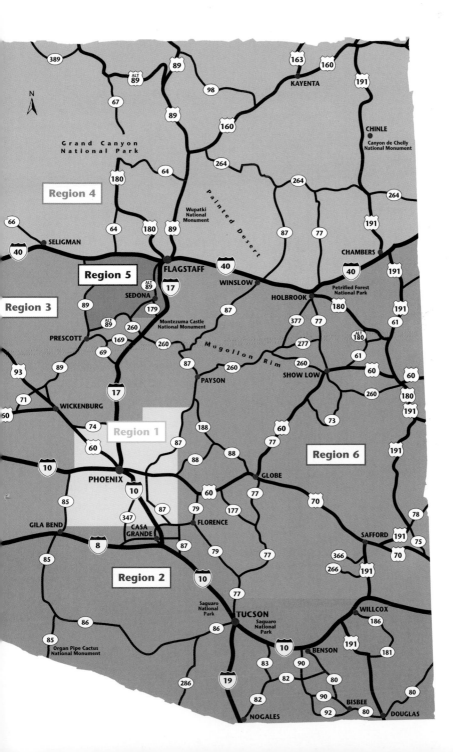

Preface

Arizona is known for its natural desert beauty, but what often goes unrecognized is the religious beauty of this state's spiritual places. From historic Catholic churches to Navajo sacred sites, from Mormon temples to Buddhist temples, from Jewish synagogues to Muslim mosques, this state overflows with incredible places for worship.

What a theme—and what an author—for a book of this magnitude! No one is more qualified to research and lift up Arizona's holy sites than Kelly Ettenborough. She has been writing about religious subjects and events here in Arizona for almost a decade, first as a reporter for the *Mesa Tribune* and then in the same position for *The Arizona Republic*. She has covered topics ranging from the pope's 1993 Denver visit to the everyday stories that illuminate the impact of the spiritual on daily life.

So, I invite you to follow Kelly Ettenborough as she leads us to some of the most inspiring religious sites and worship centers in this beautiful state. You are in for an educational, illuminating, and enjoyable journey.

> —Dr. Paul Eppinger
> Executive Director, Arizona Interfaith Movement
> Executive Director (Ret.), Arizona Ecumenical Council

Above and opposite: Mission San Xavier del Bac, Tucson

Introduction

onfession, many religions teach, cleanses the soul. So I'll begin this book with a confession. I moved to Arizona for love. I wasn't in love with the desert or the mountains, like so many who move here, but with my fiancé. Actually, I thought Arizona's landscape paled in comparison with the overgrown beauty of southeast Missouri, where I grew up, with its vistas of flat farmland, thick forests, and the mighty Mississippi River. Even though I spent part of almost every year in Arizona as a child and teenager, I had yet to connect with the desert or the mountains.

After I moved to Arizona in 1987, I missed the bright fall leaves on the maples and oaks and the spring flowers on the dogwood trees. Once, I planned a trip back home to coincide with the peak weekend for fall foliage in Missouri, Tennessee, and Kentucky. The glorious reds, yellows, and oranges there surpassed Flagstaff's show, I thought.

Then, one early morning, a newspaper assignment took me through the desert east of metropolitan Phoenix. In March and April, wildflowers explode in the desert, especially after a wet winter. As I drove, I noticed how the rising sun made the desert glow in infinite shades of green. Hawks circled overhead and the tangy smell of creosote bush drifted through the car's open sunroof. As only sweeping desert and mountains surrounded my lone car, I realized how much I adored Arizona. I finally felt the inspiration and magic of the landscape.

When I started covering religion and spirituality nearly a decade ago, I found that the state's natural beauty fostered infinite religious expressions, from Sedona's Chapel of the Holy Cross—a church nestled between red sandstone monoliths—to the Native American tribes' reverence for Spirit in nature.

Arizona is a maverick state, a place to reinvent yourself. That was true long before 1912, when Arizona became a state on Valentine's Day, and it's true today. This mystique helps to draw new residents at a brisk rate.

Census statistics show that Arizona has been growing three times faster than other states. In the last decade, Arizona's population ballooned to 5.3 million people, an increase of 40 percent. Slightly more than half of the growth came from people relocating here from other states, while 16 percent of the growth resulted from people immigrating here from foreign countries. By 2020, Arizona will be home to 8.2 million people, growth projections show, with most of those people living in the metropolitan Phoenix area. The state—and its religious and spiritual practices—become more diverse every day.

Often, spirituality fits into that new sense of self. For me, this is why hardly a week goes by without a call to the newspaper from a recent transplant asking for a recommendation of a church, synagogue, or other religious congregation. If you are one of those callers, you know that I refrain from making recommendations because I don't know you or your specific needs. And, as a newspaper reporter with a mission of impartial and fair coverage, I'm always hesitant to single out one place in particular.

But writing a book that highlights a hundred places of all kinds throughout the state is a different project for me—an opportunity to introduce you to a variety of spiritual destinations for your own personal journey. I hope that in these pages you will find something that speaks to you, wherever you are in life.

This project was planned long before the horrific acts of September 11, 2001. In the midst of covering stories about religion and terrorism, I wondered how this book project would fit with the ensuing shift in American consciousness. But the more I wrote about people waking up to a need for spirituality and looking anew for a connection with God, whether in organized religion or on a different spiritual path, I knew this was the right time.

My wish is that you'll find what you are seeking as you explore these snapshots in words and photographs of Arizona's sanctuaries, retreats, and sacred places—and as you make your own way in the desert.

Canaan in the Desert, Phoenix

How to Use This Guide

Maybe you harbor a burning desire to learn about the vortexes, or energy centers, in Sedona, or you feel closest to God when on your knees in a beautiful and majestic Roman Catholic church. Perhaps you've wondered about the roadside shrine on US 60 near Miami, or you would like to explore the teachings of Buddhism in a friendly environment.

This book will give you a place to begin, an idea of what you can find throughout the state in religious and spiritual traditions of all kinds. From the historic to the out-of-the-way, from a group retreat to a silent night in a mountainside teepee, these are places that promote balance and harmony. My hope is that this book will be a helpful and kind companion on your spiritual journey throughout the state.

Regional Designations and Maps

Arizona divides itself geographically and by population into six regions: the Phoenix area, Tucson and southern Arizona, Prescott and west-central Arizona, the Grand Canyon area in northern Arizona, the Sedona area, and east-central Arizona. The Arizona map on pages 8–9 depicts these six regions. Each region, or chapter, opens with its own map showing the numbered sanctuaries, retreats, and sacred places discussed in the chapter. Regions are color-coded throughout the book for quick reference.

Phoenix and its surrounding suburbs contain more people—3 million and growing every day—than any other part of the state. Here, you will find sanctuaries of peace in the midst of a busy city with religious expressions from around the world. Early Spanish and Mexican influences strongly shaped Tucson and southern Arizona, evident in such missions as San Xavier del Bac and Tumacácori. Prescott serves as a church-camp mecca, and the shining jewels of central and western Arizona include the Shrine of St. Joseph of the Mountains in Yarnell and the Montezuma Well, a Native American sacred site of creation. The Grand Canyon inspires everyone, from Christians who praise God for creating such an awesome sight to the Havasupai who live in the bottom of the canyon near turquoise waterfalls. Sedona is known far and wide as a New Age haven. Eastern Arizona's claim to fame is its Mormon pioneer heritage, and Snowflake is home to the state's newest Mormon temple. And throughout the state, ancient and modern Native American spirituality permeates the rhythms of life.

Mission in the Sun, Tucson

Clearly, with such a rich cultural and religious heritage, Arizona offers more spiritual destinations than these pages could ever contain. But here are some starting points for experiencing the spiritual and religious range that defines Arizona.

What Are Sanctuaries, Retreats, and Sacred Places?

Within these six regions, the destinations are designated as sanctuaries, retreats, or sacred places. On the regional maps, sanctuaries are depicted in red, retreats in purple, and sacred places in gold.

Many destinations could be considered a sanctuary, retreat, and sacred place all rolled into one. But for the purposes of this book, "sanctuaries" are usually places where religious services are held, such as active churches, mosques, or synagogues. They are places to spend the day, as overnight accommodations are not available.

Typically, "retreats" offer everything that sanctuaries do, but with expanded programs and overnight accommodations. Stays can range from one night to three months or more. Retreats also might be sacred places with accommodations, from campsites to hotel-style facilities.

"Sacred places" speak to the more spiritual, less structured experience. Energy vortexes, natural features, and places sacred to Native Americans are examples, as are the Garden of Gethsemane in Tucson and the gardens at the COFCO Chinese Cultural Center in Phoenix.

Out of respect to Arizona's tribes, the Native American sacred sites covered are ones that are most accessible to the public, and for the most part, do not require a long hike to reach. Many tribal sacred sites are closed to non-tribal visitors as a way to safeguard the practices and keep holy sites from being

vandalized or co-opted by others. For example, the Tohono O'odham consider I'ito's Cave in southern Arizona's Baboquivari Mountains as a sacred site related to their creation story. The campgrounds and picnic areas are open, and the mountains can be hiked, but the cave is strictly off-limits to those outside the tribe. Please respect such restrictions. In Sedona and in other places, New Age retreat centers with Native American spiritual directors offer insight into such religious traditions as sweat lodges, vision quests, and medicine wheels, so you can experience these practices without going where you are not invited.

Site Listings

Written to stand alone, the entries offer the basics: contact information, location, a brief description, and directions. The text gives a detailed account of what you can expect to find at each place, with prices, hours, and explanations about the beliefs and practices espoused there. Whether you're going to a particular part of the state, or you're interested solely in sacred places or retreats, you can flip through the book and pick and choose.

Planning Your Trip

The information in this book is as complete and up-to-date as possible, but always call ahead to make your specific plans, particularly for destinations that will take you far away from home. (Note that, except for the Navajo Nation, Arizona does not observe Daylight Saving Time.) Ownership, prices, and hours can change. Many retreat centers book weeks in advance. Some places welcome spur-of-the-moment visits, but others, especially retreats, cannot accommodate guests at the last minute.

Be patient. For many of the kind folks at these sites, answering the phone does not rank as a high priority in a day of prayer, work, and solitude. Neither does returning phone calls within the same day.

Although some places have accommodations that rival the fanciest of resorts, others offer more rustic sleeping arrangements such as bunk beds or sleeping bags on the floor. Most retreat centers do not have phones, televisions, or computer access in the rooms. Keep in mind that you are not going on a vacation but on a quest for spiritual introspection and growth, where such trappings will hinder these goals. If you're not an outdoorsy person and dislike sharing a bathroom with strangers, a church camp might not be for you.

Opposite: Santa Rita Abbey, Sonoita

Remember to be a good guest. Leave cellular phones and pagers silent, or better yet, in your car. Children and animals are not always welcome, so please find out before bringing your entire entourage. Although not every locale in this book is one of silent prayer and contemplation, these are holy places, sought out for the solitude and inspiration they provide, so refrain from disrupting others who arrived there before you.

Traveling in Arizona

Although Arizona's urban areas hum with activity, the state has vast stretches of road, some unpaved, where cars seldom go. Often, there's no gas station in sight. Make sure someone knows your travel plans, especially if you are traveling alone, and check in with him or her when you get back.

Don't drive through a flooded wash. Ever. Don't take your car off a paved road unless you know for sure where the road goes and that your vehicle is capable of such a trip. The same is true for roads covered with ice and snow, as you might find in northern Arizona.

Take a detailed road map with you, such as the *Arizona Road & Recreation Atlas* by Benchmark Maps. A cellular phone can prove handy in an emergency, but don't depend on it alone because your phone might not have service in many mountain and canyon areas.

Always carry water, a minimum of 1 gallon per person, per day. Also bring food such as granola bars, but water is most important. Drink plenty of water when the weather is warm and while you are engaging in outdoor activities because, in some cases, dehydration and heat exhaustion can prove fatal.

Pack extra blankets in your trunk because, even during the scorching summer, overnight temperatures in the open desert drop dramatically. Outdoors experts often recommend lightweight and compact "space blankets," which can be used to make shade during the day and to create warmth at night. These blankets reflect light, another plus should a search-and-rescue team need to find you.

Pack flashlights. Stay with your car if you are lost. A vehicle is larger and much easier to spot from the air than a single person.

As a newspaper reporter, I have written and read too many stories about people who underestimate the harsh realities of desert and mountain environments. Sometimes they die. Please don't become one of those people. Be careful out there, and have a safe and fulfilling journey.

Opposite: Yaqui deer dancer sculpture at Ted De Grazia's art gallery, Mission in the Sun, Tucson

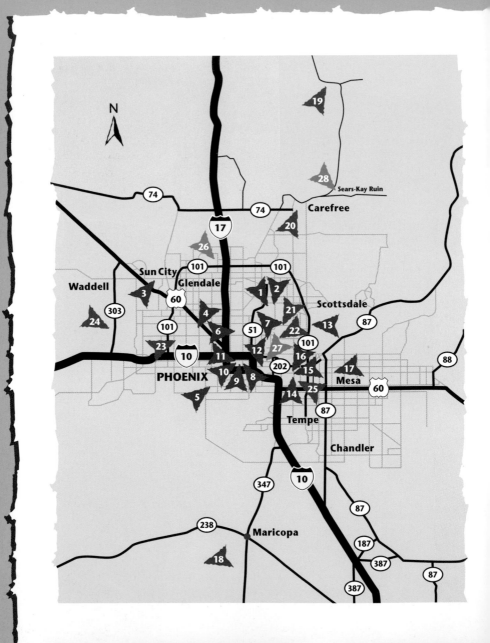

*W*ith such a diversity of experiences available, the metropolitan Phoenix area—otherwise known as the Valley of the Sun—makes for an ideal place to explore and develop your spirituality. Here, you can surround yourself with angels in Sun City, visit historic churches that still nurture vibrant faith, relax at a serene Zen retreat in a college town neighborhood, or stand in awe before the Mesa Temple, one of the world's largest and oldest Mormon temples.

A yoga retreat sounds inviting. A walk in the desert engenders peace and a sense of purpose as you follow the last days of Jesus and listen to the sounds of quail families and a bubbling fountain.

People from around the world have planted roots in this valley, built houses of worship, and influenced the local culture. Perhaps it's the yearning to reinvent the self that pervades this place of 70-degree January days, but here you will find opportunities for spiritual growth unavailable in the average American town. From old churches to mystical journeys, the Valley of the Sun restores everyone's soul.

Sanctuaries

1. Canaan in the Desert

Evangelical Sisterhood of Mary
9849 N. 40th St.
Phoenix, AZ 85028
(602) 996-4040
E-mail: marysisters@intelispan.com
www.kanaan.org/USA

The essentials of the Christian faith and the splendors of nature converge at Canaan in the Desert, a peaceful place to connect with the presence of God.

In the Garden of Jesus' Sufferings and His Resurrection, the Lutheran nuns of the Evangelical Sisterhood of Mary re-created Christ's final journey— this time set along meandering pathways in the natural desert of northern Phoenix. They also created a true sanctuary of quiet in a busy city. Nothing disturbs the silence, not the quail families scampering across the desert, nor the sisters working in the garden. This is a place to be alone with God and contemplate the mystery of the faith and of your life.

These words from Mother Basilea Schlink, the order's cofounder, greet you at the garden's entrance: "Pour out your heart to God your father. He understands you better than you do and knows best how to help you."

The layout of the garden mirrors the end of Jesus' life, but not in the fashion of the traditional Roman Catholic Stations of the Cross. Wooden

Location: About 20 minutes north of downtown Phoenix.

Description: A solitary place of prayer and reflection in a Christian setting on 10 acres of natural desert near the Phoenix Mountain Preserve.

How to get there: From AZ 51 (Squaw Peak Parkway), go east on Shea Boulevard (Exit 9). Drive for 0.8 mile and turn right (south) on North 40th Street. Drive for 0.4 mile. The entrance to Canaan in the Desert is on the left (east) side of the road and the sign is small.

and concrete benches are scattered throughout the property, perfect for prayer or reading. The Fountain of the Father's Goodness symbolizes God's overflowing love, and mosaic tiles spell out his attributes—"merciful," "gracious"—around the fountain's edges.

Large, sculptured reliefs, set in shelters, mark most of the points along the path. The journey begins with the sleeping disciples and ends with the resurrection, a realistic and almost life-size depiction of a risen Jesus, with the wounds evident in his hands and feet. At the Calvary scene, the bright sky outlines three empty crosses.

Completed in 1983, the garden celebrates the presence of God among his people, the sisters say, and illustrates the forgiveness of sins through Jesus. A simple chapel seats about 30. Guests may attend daily prayer and special services or wander the grounds unattended during daylight hours, free of charge. The crushed granite paths, bordered with rocks, are wheelchair accessible. The sisters make themselves available to anyone who needs spiritual direction, but only on request.

Mother Basilea Schlink and Mother Martyria Madauss founded the Evangelical Sisterhood of Mary in 1947 in Germany as a response to the devastation of war and the horror of the Nazi regime. The young women survived the September 11, 1944, air raid of Darmstadt that left 12,000 dead. After an encounter with God that night, they joined together to spread a message of love and reconciliation.

In 1966, the sisters came to Phoenix. They first bought property in central Phoenix, but eventually moved to the 10 acres adjacent to the Phoenix Mountain Preserve. Here, the sisters created a place to find solitude and to reflect on God's goodness, mercy, and faithfulness.

This garden, though, does not resemble the lush gardens and lake of the original, in Darmstadt, Germany. That Kanaan, the German spelling for Canaan, was so named because its land, like the Promised Land, was acquired by faith alone. The sisters maintain outposts around the world, and about half have gardens. This is the order's only American branch.

2. Temple Beth Israel

10460 N. 56th St.
Scottsdale, AZ 85253
(480) 951-0323
www.templebethisrael.com

Location: Scottsdale/Phoenix border.
Description: Arizona's oldest and largest Reform synagogue.
How to get there: From AZ 51 (Squaw Peak Parkway), go east on Shea Boulevard (Exit 9) and drive 3 miles to 56th Street. The synagogue is on the southwest corner of 56th Street and Shea Boulevard.

Temple Beth Israel, the largest and oldest Reform congregation in Arizona, defines itself through its past as well as its present. The synagogue connects its members back to more than 4,000 years of tradition in the Jewish faith. In Reform fashion, it honors tradition and ritual but allows for modern conveniences, such as driving your car, rather than walking, to services on the Sabbath.

With a strong membership that includes about 1,000 families, the synagogue today serves as a center of Jewish culture in the Valley of the Sun, and its members are committed to taking leadership roles in the community. The congregation often donates money and time to causes both Jewish and non-Jewish in effort to make the Valley—and the world—a better place for others.

The religion, according to the synagogue's rabbi, goes beyond just coming in on Friday, Saturday, and Sunday to say nice prayers and adorn ourselves with righteousness. The religion means to go out into the community. The standard is compassion.

The first Jewish pioneers came to Arizona during its territorial days in the mid-1800s as the "Great Western Expansion" brought settlers looking for gold, for land, and for opportunity. By 1870, the small farming community of Phoenix, near the then-flowing Salt River, had become an attractive place to homestead. The early Jewish settlers wanted to worship here as well, and by 1920, Temple Beth Israel was founded in downtown Phoenix, miles and years away from its current location in the northeast Valley.

By 1955, Phoenix boasted 3,000 Jewish families and two temples, Temple Beth Israel and Beth El Congregation. Temple Beth Israel moved from the central Phoenix corridor to its home at 56th Street and Shea Boulevard in 1997. The 45,000-square-foot facility includes a sanctuary that seats 500 and a chapel for 300.

Fused glass surrounded by colored glass adorns the ark, the place in the front of the synagogue where the Torahs (the Holy Scriptures) are stored. The Torah, written in Hebrew on a long scroll wrapped around two rods, comprises the first five books of the Old Testament.

Temple Beth Israel houses one of the largest Judaica libraries—20,000 volumes—in the Southwest. The library, which is open to the congregation and to the public, began humbly in 1942 as one shelf holding 60 books. The small tables and chairs in the children's section make it inviting for the little ones. The atmosphere recalls that of a small, neighborhood branch of a public library. All of its contents, though, are Jewish.

The Sylvia Plotkin Judaica Museum showcases exhibits of Jewish culture and religious practice from around the world. The museum has a small replica of the Western Wall, or Wailing Wall, the only remaining part of the original temple of Jerusalem destroyed by the Romans in the first century. As at the original Western Wall, visitors to the museum write their prayers to God and tuck them into the wall. Volunteers take the notes to Israel and place them inside the ancient crevices of the real Western Wall. The museum also displays historic Torahs: a 300-year-old Torah from Egypt and another that endured through the Holocaust.

Temple Beth Israel houses a preschool and a large religious school, and offers numerous educational programs for children and adults. The synagogue has added programs in recent years that embrace the changing family structure with sincerity, warmth, and caring, and attract Jews who have not affiliated themselves with a synagogue.

The synagogue owns Camp Charles Pearlstein in the Prescott National Forest, the only Jewish camp among the numerous church and secular camps in the area. The camp's outdoor synagogue nestled among the pines makes for a worshipful atmosphere. During the summer, youths from throughout the Southwest attend the camp, and other groups use the facility for fall, winter, and spring retreats.

3. St. Clement of Rome Catholic Church

15800 Del Webb Blvd.
Sun City, AZ 85351
(623) 974-5867

A heavenly host surrounds visitors to St. Clement of Rome Catholic Church in Sun City. Julie's Angel Haven, one of three angel museums in the United States, is located off the parish hall in a meeting room.

But don't just think of this setup as a museum in a meeting room. More than 1,000 angels showcase the possibilities of celestial beings in both inspiring and funny ways. The angels appeal equally to traditional religious sensibilities and to the more spiritual. Perhaps, if you listen closely, they will burst into a song of praise or bring out the quiet prayer in your heart.

For seven decades, Julie Chestna, a parishioner at St.

Clement, has collected angels. She purchased her first as a teenager, with money earned from her first job. As she traveled the world with her husband, she always brought home angels. When, in her 80s, she moved to a smaller home, she donated the majority of her angels to the church.

The angels, large and small, represent the spectrum of the human imagination for these creatures of light. The classic beauty of fine porcelain Lladro angels from Spain gives way to the quaint kitsch of the angel hand-soap dispenser by the room's small sink. Modern-art angels share space with needlepoint angels. Baby angels nap and gray-haired "retired"

Location: Sun City, a retirement community about 40 minutes northwest of downtown Phoenix.

Description: Roman Catholic church with one of three angel museums in the United States and a courtyard dedicated to the Rosary.

How to get there: From Loop 101, go west on Bell Road (Exit 14) for 3 miles. Turn left (south) on Del Webb Boulevard and drive for 0.7 mile. The church is on the right (west) side of the road.

angels play bingo. An angel stands guard at the Vatican and hand-carved wooden angels hail from a London antique shop.

Julie Chestna's affinity for angels started at her birth. She wasn't breathing and the doctor pronounced her dead. Her mother, who had lost two children already, held her tightly as she prayed and cried. Chestna credits angels for the miracle that turned her mother's grief into joy.

St. Clement's also provides a place for quiet prayer in its courtyard dedicated to the Rosary. Sun City's status as a retirement community makes the statues of a young Mary with Jesus' grandparents, St. Joachim and St. Anne, particularly appropriate for the Rosary courtyard. Benches surround the statues and Bougainvillea vines bloom red most of the year. The garden is dedicated to unborn children.

The courtyard is open during the day, and the museum opens at about 1 p.m., after the noon Mass on the first Sunday of the month and on Wednesday mornings. You can arrange group and individual showings by calling the church office.

4. Arizona Buddhist Temple

4142 W. Clarendon Ave.
Phoenix, AZ 85019
(602) 278-0036
http://aztec.asu.edu/worship/azbuddhist/

*O*nce, commercial buildings and vehicular traffic did not encroach upon the Arizona Buddhist Temple in west Phoenix. The tiny garden tucked between the temple's modest buildings might not be quite as serene as the days when fields surrounded the complex, before growth caught up with the congregation. However, the temple is worth noting for its part in Arizona history as the first Buddhist congregation here, and for its importance in today's worship. It also celebrates culture through such

events as the Obon Festival in June, when colorful Japanese lanterns transform the white buildings and gravel parking lot for an ancient Japanese rite honoring the dead and the interconnectedness of all life.

Near the pagoda is the statue of Shinran Shonin, who founded the Jodo Shinshu sect in 13th-century Japan. He emphasized the practice of Buddhism for ordinary people as part of their daily lives, rather than only for those who went to study the religion in isolated places.

Japanese immigrants founded this congregation in the 1930s as the Arizona Buddhist Church, affiliated with Buddhist Churches in America. During World

Location: West of downtown Phoenix.

Description: Arizona's oldest Buddhist congregation; adheres to the Jodo Shinshu sect's practices.

How to get there: From I-10, go north on 43rd Avenue (Exit 140). Go 2 miles and turn right (east) on Clarendon Avenue.

War II, the temple closed because leaders and the minister were sent to internment camps.

The experience of the internment camps and continuing racism strengthened the resolve of Japanese-Americans to synthesize with American culture through the trappings of the church. Unlike the practitioners of the Jodo Shinshu sect of Buddhism in Japan, the Japanese-Americans worship on Sunday mornings, with pews, an organ, hymnals, and a spiritual leader called "reverend." But the elaborate altar features Amida Buddha, the Buddha of infinite light and infinite life, rather than a cross.

In the 1990s, the Arizona congregation was among the first in its denomination to recognize its heritage by changing its name from church to temple. Worship still takes place on Sunday mornings because that's most convenient for everyone, and the spiritual leader is still a reverend. But the congregation today now focuses on proudly sharing its spiritual diversity and heritage rather than trying to blend in.

Buddhism is a spiritual path to seek wisdom and enlightenment, thousands of years older than Christianity. Non-Japanese members also belong to the temple, which welcomes anyone interested in learning more about the Jodo Shinshu sect of Buddhism. Services are in Japanese and English.

5. New Age Community Church

6418 S. 39th Ave.
Phoenix, AZ 85041
(602) 237-3213
E-mail: rodgers@aznewage.com
www.aznewage.com

*T*hose who subscribe to New Age or pagan spiritual beliefs usually don't join churches. But on Sundays at the New Age Community Church, maybe a dozen people attend services at this modest, out-of-the-way house that became the organizing hub for Phoenix's New Age community 30 years ago. Sunday morning services aren't the main activity here, but for those who find comfort in such weekly meetings, the format would resemble a Protestant service, with music, communion, and teaching. The congregation also meditates.

The church community strives to help people move beyond the confusion of religion to a higher consciousness and find the prime truth behind all religions, says the Rev. John Rodgers, founder and bishop of the church. Rodgers also publishes *The Omega Directory*, a monthly newspaper filled with resources and local, national, and international stories of interest to the alternative spiritual community.

Location: Southwest Phoenix.

Description: A community of likeminded New Age believers that invites others to explore new spiritual avenues through a Protestant-style service.

How to get there: From I-10, go south on 35th Avenue (Exit 141). Go almost 5 miles, turn right (west) on Southern Avenue, then go left (south) on 39th Avenue. The church is about five blocks south of Southern Avenue on the right (west) side of 39th Avenue.

The church members study a variety of teachings from the scriptures of world religions to magick, from *The Course in Miracles* to the healing secrets of ancient shamans. It views all scripture as divinely inspired when taken in proper context. For many years, the New Age church has offered a seminary program, through which Rodgers has taught 1,000 ministers. In any given semester, about 100 people from around the country are enrolled in the program.

Church teachings hold that the purpose of life is happiness, and focus on love rather than guilt. They diverge from the traditional Christian view that God sent Jesus to die and rise again in atonement for the sins of humankind. The congregation believes in God as the "one eternal reality," the Earth as the "great matriarch" and life source, and that we dwell simultaneously in spiritual and physical dimensions.

According to its written statements, the church also espouses these beliefs: (1) God is perfect and does not make mistakes. All his creations are perfect, too, including Adam and Eve, who being perfect could not sin. Because they did not sin, God did not murder his son to atone for it. (2) God loves us perfectly. God is not going to condemn us at some mythological judgment day. Nor has he created a terrible place in which to torment us for eternity. (3) God is unchanging and the universe reflects his will. God has never written a book or established a church or priesthood to operate on his behalf. You do not have to belong to any particular organization to please God, nor do you have to avoid meat, alcohol, or sexual relations to get into heaven.

The church has started two other congregations to serve those who live east and west of Phoenix: The Blessed Circle, or the Eastside New Age Community Church, and the West Valley New Age Community Church. Rodgers believes that eventually, organized religion will end, and people will go back to following gurus and teachers in small groups, like in the old days. "In the meantime," he explains, "we're holding out as a church."

6. Asbury United Methodist Church

1601 W. Indian School Rd.
Phoenix, AZ 85015
(602) 279-2369
www.aplaceforallpeople.com

Once upon a time, Asbury United Methodist Church was a graying congregation. The members were open to allowing a small gay and lesbian group to meet in the small chapel on its property. The congregation then voted in favor of inviting the group to join Asbury. The vote put Asbury on the path to becoming one of the most diverse congregations in the Valley—a place where no one cares about gay or straight, just about serving and loving God together as a family.

The church's core values are "being intentionally inclusive; nurturing souls; exercising bold, courageous leadership; putting Christ's love into action; and encouraging people to use their unique gifts in ministry." The church encourages theological exploration and, unlike scriptural literalists, teaches that "the Bible is a window through which we see God and better understand ourselves—and not a static, inerrant textbook."

These questions are asked of potential members: Will you love God with your whole heart? Will you love your neighbor as generously as you

Location: Central Phoenix.

Description: One of a handful of United Methodist churches in the United States that is a welcoming congregation for gays and lesbians.

How to get there: From I-17, go east on Indian School Road (Exit 202) for about 1 mile. The church is on the southwest corner of 16th Street and Indian School Road.

love yourself? Will you accept Jesus as your savior and live as a disciple of Christ? Will you live your life with generosity and hope?

The congregation is active with ministries as diverse as a handbell choir to a monthly luncheon for people living with HIV and AIDS. Asbury has hosted such nationally known speakers as the Rev. Jimmy Creech, who the United Methodist Church tried for performing a same-sex wedding in 1998, and the Rev. Mel White, an evangelical pastor and ghostwriter for Billy Graham, Jerry Falwell, and Oliver North. Author of the best-selling autobiography *Stranger at the Gate: To Be Gay and Christian in America*, White came out as a gay man and began working for the rights of "God's gay and lesbian children."

In 1996, the congregation voted by a 92 percent margin to become the first reconciling congregation in Phoenix, a designation meaning that it invited anyone to join in church life. Asbury was the 112th of the 36,000 United Methodist churches in the United States to take this step. But in 1999, the denomination ruled that a local congregation couldn't identify itself with any movement. Asbury, however, has remained a welcoming congregation for all people.

7. Holy Trinity Greek Orthodox Cathedral

1973 E. Maryland Ave.
Phoenix, AZ 85016
(602) 264-7863
www.holytrinityphx.org

The gleaming white dome topped with the cross competes with the nearby Phoenix Mountain Preserve in beauty. No wonder the parishioners of Holy Trinity Greek Orthodox Cathedral call it "the jewel of the desert." And inside, the church really takes your breath away with more than 10,000 square feet of faceted glass icons.

Holy Trinity is a leader in maintaining an Orthodox presence in the Valley, with its popular Greek Festival, Greek language classes for children and adults, and outreach efforts. More than 800 families constitute the parish.

The cathedral is the mother church of the other Greek Orthodox churches spread throughout the Valley. In 1923, 10 men organized the first Greek Orthodox congregation in Phoenix. As the community grew and

Location: North Phoenix.

Description: The mother church of the Valley of the Sun's other Greek Orthodox cathedrals.

How to get there: From AZ 51 (Squaw Peak Parkway), go east on Glendale Avenue (Exit 5). Go right (south) on 20th Street for 0.5 mile, then right (west) on Maryland Avenue. The cathedral is on the left (south) side of the street.

expanded in central Phoenix, the parish needed more room. So, in 1972, the land that now makes up its current location was purchased. The new cathedral first welcomed worshipers on Palm Sunday, April 18, 1976. Later, an education building, library, and chapel were added. The church property also boasts a sports complex with a softball field, tennis/basketball court, and sand volleyball court.

Most Orthodox churches in America mix English and the congregation's native language in services. In Holy Trinity's main sanctuary, the worship service is conducted in 70 percent English and 30 percent Greek; an English-language service is held in the chapel for children.

Throughout the world, more than 300 million people are Orthodox Christians. In the United States, about 1.5 million people are Greek Orthodox. Although Orthodoxy does not send missionaries out to spread the word, the church has drawn more people in recent years because they view its structure and worship as akin to that of early Christianity. The church liturgy appeals to all the senses, with incense, chanting, singing, and communion, all in beautiful surroundings.

The Orthodox church has ancient roots. It follows the decree set by the First Ecumenical Council of the undivided Church at Nicaea, Asia Minor, held in A.D. 325. Therefore, Orthodox Christians set holidays according to the Julian calendar, so Easter and Christmas typically fall later than the holidays set by the Gregorian calendar, which most churches use today. Orthodox beliefs resemble those of other Christian traditions, with the exception that, according to its teachings, the church has preserved the Apostles' faith intact. Practitioners of Orthodoxy believe in the real presence of Jesus in the Holy Eucharist—the bread and wine of communion—offered for eternal life and forgiveness of sins. Icons are treated with special reverence for the person they represent but are not worshipped. The sacredness of the subject matter differentiates icons from other paintings and images. Orthodox Christians believe that Christ himself made the first icon, his image in his burial cloth, known as the Shroud of Turin.

8. Trinity Episcopal Cathedral

100 W. Roosevelt St.
Phoenix, AZ 85003
(602) 254-7126
www.trinitycathedral.com

*T*rinity Episcopal Cathedral celebrates much these days as the congregation reclaims its historic position as a center for worship, learning, and culture. Faced with a deteriorating neighborhood and declining attendance, the church could have gone the way of many urban congregations that sold their buildings and headed for the suburbs.

But the roots of this cathedral grow deeply in central Phoenix. The congregation formed in the Arizona Territory in 1888, and the Spanish Colonial-style cathedral was completed in 1921. At its peak in 1948, Trinity had 2,000 members. By 1990, attendance had plummeted to about 80. Instead of giving up, the congregation decided to "resurrect" the cathedral in downtown Phoenix.

Believing that too few beautiful places exist in the world, the congregation felt called to make the cathedral an offering to the community. The stained-glass windows inspire lofty prayers. The labyrinth in the courtyard brings you back to earth to focus on the present as you walk the ever-narrowing circle. Sounds of traffic disappear. Some pray, some chant, some sing, some silently walk the labyrinth.

Location: Downtown Phoenix.

Description: A recently restored historic cathedral with a diverse congregation and community outreach programs.

How to get there: From I-10, go south on Seventh Street (Exit 145). Go right (west) on Roosevelt Street and drive 0.5 mile. The cathedral is just west of Central Avenue on the right (north) side of Roosevelt Street.

Some church members puzzled over the labyrinth, wondering if this New Age trend belonged on the grounds of a Christian church. But the labyrinth actually got its start in the Middle Ages as a way to meditate and pray to God. Trinity's labyrinth is a paved replica of the one at the famed French cathedral Notre-Dame de Chartres.

A multimillion-dollar restoration effort returned the cathedral to its original splendor, and it has since become a special venue for concerts. A Schantz pipe organ now serves as a centerpiece for the almost acoustically perfect building, which architects designed so voices could carry to the back of the room without the use of a microphone.

Trinity, a reinvigorated church in a neighborhood that is also enjoying urban revitalization efforts, now sees about 350 people on weekends for worship. It offers two different types of service: the traditional Holy Eucharist and Taizé, during which the congregation participates in a contemplative style of prayer through readings, meditative silence, and singing chantlike refrains. The congregation ranks among the more diverse in the Valley, with young and old, gay and straight, and people of all races worshiping together and bettering their community through a wide variety of social service programs.

9. Immaculate Heart of Mary Catholic Church

909 E. Washington St.
Phoenix, AZ 85034
(602) 253-6129

*M*ore than any other Catholic church in the Phoenix metro area, worship at Immaculate Heart of Mary Catholic Church evokes the style of parishes in Mexico. The church, where Masses are held in English and Spanish, is the Mexico national parish of the Roman Catholic Diocese of Phoenix.

Both recent immigrants and fourth- and fifth-generation Mexican-American families call the parish home. Those who are adjusting to life in a foreign land feel at home here. The church draws members from the surrounding neighborhoods and from throughout the Valley who want to worship in the style traditional to Mexico, in which devotion to Our Lady of Guadalupe plays a key role.

Pope Pius XI signed the decree on December 12, 1924, to create Immaculate Heart of Mary to serve the growing Spanish-speaking population in Phoenix. The members of the congregation, who had been worshiping in the basement at what is now St. Mary's Basilica, broke ground on their own church in 1928. They raised $135,000 to build the church, school, and rectory. The property is on the National Register of Historic Places and on Phoenix's Historic Register.

Location: Downtown Phoenix.

Description: The Mexico national parish of the Roman Catholic Diocese of Phoenix.

How to get there: From I-10, go south on Seventh Street (Exit 145). After 1 mile, go left (east) on Jefferson Street, past Ninth Street. Go left (north) on 11th Street and then left (west) on Washington Street. The church is on the left (south) at Ninth and Washington streets. The back of the church parking lot also is accessible from Jefferson Street.

Immaculate Heart of Mary Catholic Church has had its share of heartbreak over the years. Most recently, the church caught fire in the early morning hours after the last Mass on Palm Sunday, April 17, 2000. Arson, an electrical short, and a candle left burning were considered as causes, but none was conclusively pinpointed as the source of the fire. Firefighters were able to save only the shrine with the Blessed Sacrament.

On Palm Sunday 2002, two years after the fire, the bishop of the diocese consecrated and blessed the restored church to much rejoicing and fanfare. Mariachi music enlivened the rededication festivities, as it does during special Masses.

The $3 million project returned Immaculate Heart to its original design and colors, with some changes, such as the installation of a baptismal font suitable for full immersion. The wooden pews resemble the previous ones, and the murals depicting the 16th-century miracle of Our Lady of Guadalupe's appearance before peasant boy Juan Diego have been restored. Now back to its former glory, Immaculate Heart will continue to serve as a cultural and religious bastion for the Mexican-American community.

10. St. Mary's Basilica

231 N. Third St.
Phoenix, AZ 85004
(602) 252-7651

The Mission Revival architecture of St. Mary's Basilica provides a graceful counterpoint to the high-rises and sports arenas of downtown Phoenix. The bells ringing the hours add music to the sounds of traffic.

Priests say daily Mass at the church, and doors often open during the day for private prayers. Inside, the church is traditional with rows of pews, high ceilings, and inspiring art. Emil Frei of St. Louis designed and installed the stained-glass windows, in place since 1914 and donated by some of Phoenix's leading citizens of the day.

The Valley's oldest Catholic parish, St. Mary's began as a small adobe building on its present site in 1881 and has been staffed by Franciscan Friars since 1895. According to the church's historian, it was built because the priest grew tired of the three-day journey across the desert from Florence,

Location: Downtown Phoenix.

Description: The oldest Catholic church in the Valley and mother church of other area Catholic churches; provides a historic and reverent experience.

How to get there: From I-10, go south on Seventh Street (Exit 145) for almost 1 mile to Monroe Street. Go right (west) and continue 0.25 mile to Third Street. The basilica is on the right (north) side of the street.

just to say Mass in a private home. Today, St. Mary's anchors the middle of downtown, but at the turn of the last century, the church marked Phoenix's northern edge.

Construction on the present building began in 1902. Catholics in Phoenix centered their lives around St. Mary's, and until the 1920s, Catholic churches throughout the Valley started as its mission congregations.

In the 1980s, the church suffered from declining inner-city attendance, and plans included a renovation that would have destroyed its historic significance. Instead, Father Warren Rousse undertook a restoration project to maintain the historic integrity of this sacred place in the middle of a growing city.

St. Mary's is now listed on the national and state historic registers. In 1985, the Vatican designated the church the 32nd minor basilica in the United States, an honor reserved for churches of unusual artistic and historic merit. During his visit to Phoenix in 1987, Pope John Paul II made his first official stop at St. Mary's.

11. First Institutional Baptist Church

1141 E. Jefferson St.
Phoenix, AZ 85034
(602) 258-1998

*F*rom its humble beginnings funded by a Sunday-school collection of 10 cents, First Institutional Baptist Church in Phoenix evolved into a state powerhouse for civil and human rights. The church, although not the oldest African-American congregation in the state, historically has served as a gathering place for the community. When the Rev. Dr. Martin Luther King Jr. was assassinated, people began showing up at the church, says senior pastor the Rev. Dr. Warren Stewart Sr. In May 2001, the church held the funeral of the Rev. Leon Sullivan, whose principles for ethical business conduct helped to dismantle South African apartheid. And on September 11, 2001, people of color converged at First Institutional for prayer in the wake of the terrorist attacks on the World Trade Center and Pentagon.

Location: Downtown Phoenix.

Description: A historically African-American church with lively worship; members have fought for civil and state rights and reached out to help the homeless and hurting.

How to get there: From I-10, go south on Seventh Street (Exit 145). After 1 mile on Seventh Street, go left (east) on Jefferson Street, a one-way street; the church is on the south side of the street at 11th Street.

The 3,000-member congregation commutes from the suburbs to its downtown church, a beacon for the homeless and down-and-out. When other congregations moved ministries and locations to the suburbs as people left the downtown core, First Institutional decided to maintain its urban facility.

The congregation began an expansion and renovation project in 1991 that will culminate in late 2003 with the opening of the Hope Center, a multipurpose gymnasium facility for member use and for ministry expansion. The $4.2 million center will have a combination gymnasium and auditorium, along with showers, a full-size kitchen, and classrooms for youths to senior adults. The Hope Center will augment the church's already plentiful social-service ministries to the homeless and poor. Clothes, emergency food, and hygiene kits are handed out each month, and more than 80 church ministries—from volunteers who check in daily with seniors and the homebound to a church-run home for teenage mothers—are staffed almost exclusively by church volunteers.

The church first organized in 1905, during Arizona's territorial days, as Second Baptist Church. Members met in a home at 21 E. Madison St. The founding members were either former slaves or children of slaves, explains church historian Annette Smith Willis. They could read and write and kept good records about the church—such as that first Sunday-school collection—but not about themselves, Willis says.

In the days after slavery and the Emancipation Proclamation, many blacks came to Arizona seeking new lives away from the South. Many were Baptists. In northern Arizona, one out of three cowboys was black. Other African-Americans were teachers, railroad workers, and soldiers.

The church's first building was located at Fifth and East Jefferson streets. Members agreed at an October 1908 business meeting to donate $1 each prayer meeting night to a future building fund. From 1919 to 1924, as the congregation outgrew its building, worship took place in a tent. Then, in 1925, the new, larger, stucco building was dedicated. In 1927, the church changed its name to the Colored Baptist Church.

The name changed again in 1951 to First Institutional Baptist Church as a symbol of growing black pride, says Willis. The church continued to outgrow its property and, in 1963, the congregation moved east a few blocks to its present location. A large historical marker across from Bank One Ballpark pinpoints the original church site at Fifth and East Jefferson.

The church is affiliated with both the American Baptist Churches and the National Baptist Convention, USA, one of the country's oldest and largest African-American religious organizations. Today's membership also includes Native Americans, Caucasians, and Hispanics, and a Spanish-speaking congregation meets on the property. The nationally renowned senior pastor, the Rev. Dr. Warren Stewart Sr., enjoys a reputation as one of the best preachers in the country. He works with the civic, governmental, and religious leadership in the Valley, and with the National Baptist Convention, USA. Worship is lively and uplifting, and Stewart's sermons are dynamic and inspired.

12. Sky Harbor Interfaith Chapel

3800 Sky Harbor Blvd.
Phoenix, AZ 85034
(602) 244-1346

Even as the United States grows more spiritually diverse, the practical application of interfaith worship remains elusive. Sky Harbor Interfaith Chapel stands as one holy place that truly succeeds as a nexus for all faiths, both individually and together. It's truly interfaith in a way that accommodates committed practitioners of major world religions as well as the spiritual person looking for serenity and comfort.

More than 35 million passengers travel through Phoenix Sky Harbor International Airport each year, making the airport the fifth busiest in the world. Those who find the small chapel will feel comfortable, no matter what their beliefs. Muslim airport employees pray toward Mecca during the day alongside Christians seeking a quiet moment with God before a trip. Off to the side, a fountain bubbles next to a single chair, likely the most serene spot in the entire airport. Thick concrete walls block out the buzzing activity of travelers and the noisy takeoffs and landings of jets.

The chapel's design welcomes everyone. Scriptures and prayer books from the world's religions line up on a shelf. A quick change of implements for worship, stored in a closet, transforms the simple space for Catholic, Protestant, Jewish, or Islamic services. The "Golden Rule" of several religions reminds visitors of the common values people share: From Christian teachings, "Do to others what you would have them do to you." From Judaism, "Love thy neighbor as thyself." And from Buddhism, "Make thine own self the measure of the others, and so abstain from causing hurt to them."

Artists Robert and Linda McCall designed the faceted glass window outside the chapel as a tribute to God and the universe. The bright colors and images of the sun, moon, and earth inspire without a nod to a particular tradition. The National Gallery of Art and the National Air and Space Museum exhibit some of Robert McCall's pieces

Location: Terminal Four, Phoenix Sky Harbor International Airport.

Description: A small chapel tucked away inside a busy airport.

How to get there: If you are flying into or out of the airport, go to Level Three of Terminal Four. The chapel is on the east end near the shoeshine stands. The airport is accessible by Loop 202 (Red Mountain Freeway) or I-10.

as part of their permanent collections, and his work for movies includes *2001: A Space Odyssey*. He created U.S. postage stamps to commemorate the accomplishments of the space program; astronauts hand-canceled his 1971 twin stamp, "Decade of Achievement," in a special action on the moon.

The pause in the bustle of travel touches those who find their way to this chapel. Visitors leave behind comments in the guest book such as: "I appreciate the quiet space for worship and liked that many religions are recognized and made to feel welcome," and "[I] just put my kids (9 and 12) on a plane. Thank you for the quiet place to pray for their trip."

The chaplaincy program at the airport offers more than a place to pray, though. The chaplain oversees a travelers' aid program that caters to those stranded at the airport and in need of a little extra help with a meal, a place to stay, or travel plans. The aid program expanded to help women and children at local domestic violence shelters by obtaining low-cost airline tickets so they could return to family in other parts of the country.

The chapel hosts a variety of worship services each weekend for both employees and passengers. An adjacent conference room awaits for multiple purposes, from employee Bible studies to Alcoholics Anonymous meetings. Once, in the most unusual request ever made to the chaplain, a couple asked if their peregrine falcon could stretch his wings in the conference room during their layover between Oregon and St. Louis. The falcon, freed from his pet carrier, swooped around the room.

One of more than 110 airport chapels worldwide, Sky Harbor's chapel has welcomed visitors since 1987. Chapels started opening in U.S. and European airports in the 1950s to meet the needs of employees who desired to worship and pray between flights on the weekends. Most major airports around the world now make space for a chapel or for weekly religious services as passengers, not just employees, discover the joy of a quiet moment to connect with the divine as they travel.

13. Glass & Garden Community Church

8620 E. McDonald Dr.
Scottsdale, AZ 85250
(480) 948-8800

In the mid-1960s, in the days before churches reached out to younger and often disillusioned audiences with casual-dress services and rock bands, members of Glass & Garden Community Church came up with an unusual outreach idea: a drive-in church. They equipped the parking lot with speakers so people who wanted to listen to the service on Sundays could listen from their cars if they preferred not to come inside.

Location: Scottsdale, northeast of Phoenix.
Description: This drive-in church provides a religious connection for people with limited mobility or those who would like to attend Christian services while traveling.
How to get there: From Loop 101, go east on McDonald Drive (Exit 45). The church is 0.5 mile east of Loop 101.

A low-power AM radio station has since replaced the clunky speakers. Each Sunday, a few cars park on the east side of the church and tune into 800 AM, even during the hot summer. A parking lot usher greets drivers and hands them a bulletin with the words of the hymns so they can join in the congregational singing. At the greeting, when the inside worshipers shake hands and say hello, those in the cars wave and honk their horns. The usher passes the collection plate through the parking lot and also serves communion—but, of course, no popcorn.

One longtime member admits to coming to church in her pajamas years ago, figuring that God didn't care, as long as she showed up. Today, she uses a cane and some days prefers not to go inside the sanctuary.

As the name suggests, the sanctuary's decor re-creates a garden. Some stained glass graces the interior, but trees and plants dominate the setting. From the parking lot, outside congregants look upon the white-domed sanctuary with a large cross and can see the lush foliage through the clear windows.

Services take place at 10 a.m. on Sundays. The church is affiliated with the Reformed Church in America.

14. Danforth Chapel

Arizona State University
University Drive and Mill Avenue
Tempe, AZ 85287
(480) 965-3570

*Y*ears ago, most churches kept open doors around the clock. A person seeking a moment of prayer and solitude just walked inside— no appointment with God required. Then crime hit so many sacred places that alarm systems replaced unlocked doors. Although it does close at night, Danforth Chapel on the Arizona State University campus recalls this time gone by for many houses of worship.

Founded in 1885 as a teachers' college with one professor and 33 students, Arizona State University has seen its attendance rise to a current 50,000 students at its Tempe campus. William H. Danforth, the founder and chairman of Ralston Purina Co., recognized the need for a spiritual center on college campuses across the country, so his foundation donated the first $5,000 to build the university's chapel in 1945. Students and community groups raised the remaining $10,000.

The chapel's plain, two-story brick exterior blends subtly with the university campus. A peace pole planted outside says in multiple languages, "May peace prevail on earth," a hint as to the purpose of the nonsectarian chapel. The words carved in stone inside since 1948 speak more directly: "Dedicated to the worship of God with the prayer that here in communion with the highest, those who enter may acquire the spiritual power to aspire nobly, adventure daringly, serve humbly."

Inside, the white-painted block walls mask the chatter of students rushing from class to class, but you can still hear the soothing rush of water from the large fountain outside on the mall. The stained-glass windows titled "Upward Soaring Flight" depict bright blue doves swirling high, taking your spirit with them. The simply appointed chapel supports religious and spiritual expressions of all kinds, and nothing distracts you from that intended communion. Students hold a variety of worship services and meetings here each week, from the evangelical Christian groups to the Eckankar practice of "Sing *HU* for God."

Location: Tempe, east of Phoenix.
Description: A quiet spot for prayer and meditation in the center of a busy university campus.
How to get there: From Loop 202 (Red Mountain Freeway), go south at Scottsdale/Rural Road (Exit 7). Go right (west) on Apache Boulevard just past McAllister Avenue and follow the signs to Visitor Parking in Structure #1. The chapel is in the middle of the campus, just southwest of the Hayden Library entrance and northwest of the Memorial Union.

The quiet place defies its own past controversy over the 4-foot-tall wooden cross that once crowned the building. The original plans called for a cross although the chapel was built as nondenominational. Believing the symbol discriminated against non-Christians, university officials asked that the cross not be included. The cross, however, remained on the project plans and topped the finished chapel. The president of the student Religious Council used a hacksaw to remove the cross before the dedication. During a renovation five years later, in 1953, the cross returned, apparently as a nod to the holidays. This time the cross stayed in place for 37 years until it blew down in a thunderstorm.

A university president restored the cross, but in the 1990s, a lawsuit brought the Christian symbol down permanently. The Arizona affiliate of the American Civil Liberties Union filed suit, claiming the cross violated the separation of church and state. The cross now resides in the university archives.

The chapel is open 7 a.m. to 9 p.m. on weekdays; weekends are by reservation only, and the university gives scheduling preference to ASU students and faculty. The chapel's capacity of 68 makes it a popular setting for an intimate wedding.

15. St. Mary's "Old Church"

All Saints Catholic Newman Center
230 E. University Dr.
Tempe, AZ 85281
(480) 967-7823
www.newman-asu.org

Although not the Valley's oldest congregation, St. Mary's "Old Church" near Arizona State University in Tempe is its oldest church building. Built by the Hispanic community, St. Mary's Church was dedicated in January 1904. Priests from St. Mary's Basilica and later Immaculate Heart of Mary Catholic Church in Phoenix served at the parish.

In 1932, Catholic students formed the Newman Club, a campus ministry, at St. Mary's Church. That year, the church also became Our Lady of Mt. Carmel Catholic Church, a new, movable parish for Tempe announced by the bishop. In 1968, Our Lady of Mt. Carmel's congregation moved into a new church building at its current location on Rural Road. The Old Church with the simple, reverent interior and red brick exterior became part of the All Saints Catholic Newman Center. The center often hosted religious activities in lieu of the Old Church, which lacked climate control and adequate space.

The church fell into disrepair in the late 1960s and 1970s, and the city of Tempe condemned the property. In a joint project between the city and the diocese, church restoration began in the 1980s, possible through a matching grant from the Arizona Heritage Fund. The beautiful stained-glass windows were restored, and in 1995, in time for the Super Bowl in nearby Sun Devil Stadium, palm trees and brickwork revived the landscaping.

The church, listed on the National Register of Historic Places, now boasts wheelchair access and heating and air conditioning. Weekly Mass is held in the church when school is in session, and weddings, exhibits, recitals, and concerts also take place there.

Location: Tempe, east of Phoenix.
Description: The oldest church still standing in the Valley of the Sun.
How to get there: From Loop 202 (Red Mountain Freeway), go south at Scottsdale/Rural Road (Exit 7) for about 1 mile. Turn right (west) on University Drive and go for 0.5 mile. The church is on the northwest corner of University Drive and College Avenue.

16. Islamic Cultural Center of Tempe

131 E. Sixth St.
Tempe, AZ 85281
(480) 894-6070
www.tempemasjid.com

In 1983, Valley Muslims built one of the first mosques in the Valley—the Islamic Cultural Center of Tempe—mostly for immigrant families and students from nearby Arizona State University. Since then, the Muslim community here has grown larger and more diverse. The mosque's membership and the enrollment at its private K–8 school represent at least 50 nationalities, along with numerous American converts. (The Valley's first mosque, Masjid Jauharatul-Islam, is in south Phoenix at 102 W. South Mountain Ave., (602) 268-6151, and has an American imam, or spiritual leader.)

Today, the Islamic Cultural Center of Tempe offers as many programs in English as in Arabic, as well as outreach classes for those interested in learning more about Islam, one of the fastest growing religions in the world. Estimated counts of Muslims in the United States range from 2 million to 7 million, a wide spread because numbers are not officially tracked via census or membership. In Arizona, the Muslim population has grown to more than 40,000, with at least half American citizens, community leaders estimate.

Muslims believe that God revealed their holy book, the Koran, to the prophet Mohammed, the last prophet of God, about 1,400 years ago. Members of the monotheistic religion believe in the other prophets of God, from Moses to Jesus, but they do not give attributes of deity to Jesus.

Location: Tempe, east of Phoenix.

Description: A multicultural mosque serving Muslims and those interested in learning more about Islam.

How to get there: From Loop 202 (Red Mountain Freeway), go south at Center Parkway/Priest Drive (Exit 6). Go south on Priest Drive for about 0.5 mile. Turn left (east) on Rio Salado Parkway and go for 1 mile, then go right (south) on Mill Avenue. After a few blocks, turn left (east) on Sixth Street. The mosque is on the corner of Sixth Street and Myrtle Avenue, just north of the Arizona State University campus.

Islam has these five pillars of faith:

- The declaration of faith that "there is no one worthy of worship except God (Allah) and Mohammed is his messenger."
- Prayer five times a day, facing Mecca.
- Fasting during the holy month of Ramadan. The fast prohibits food and beverages during daylight hours, as well as smoking, sexual relations, and evil intentions and desires.
- Zakat, giving a portion of one's income to help the poor.
- Hajj, a pilgrimage to Mecca, once in a lifetime, for those physically able to make the journey.

The Islamic Cultural Center of Tempe conducts tours and welcomes inquiries about the faith. The mosque is at its busiest during the Friday midday prayers called Jummah, during which men sit in the front and women in the back. Women typically cover their heads as a sign of modesty, and female visitors often are asked to do the same before entering the mosque. You also must remove your shoes before entering.

17. Mesa Arizona Temple

Church of Jesus Christ of Latter-day Saints
101 S. LeSueur St.
Mesa, AZ 85204
(480) 833-1211

In Arizona, more than 313,000 members of the Church of Jesus Christ of Latter-day Saints convene in churches, or meetinghouses, each week for Sunday worship and myriad other activities. They reserve the temple for the sacred ordinances that bind families and marriages together for all eternity, according to the church teachings. The church currently has more than 100 temples and 11 million members around the world.

Only members of the Mormon church in good standing with a recommend from a bishop may enter the temple. But during daylight hours, visitors may stroll, pray, and meditate on the manicured grounds, lush with year-round green grass, flowers, tall trees, benches, and a reflecting pool.

The visitors' center welcomes those who want to know more about the teachings of the church, founded in 1830 by prophet Joseph Smith in New York as the restoration of Jesus Christ's church on Earth. Smith translated the church's sacred record of Jesus' ministry in North and South America, found on gold plates in New York. The Book of Mormon is considered Scripture along with the Bible.

Inside the visitors' center stands a 10-foot-tall, Italian marble replica of Danish sculptor Bertel Thorvaldsen's statue "The Christus." Thorvaldsen created the original sculpture of the resurrected Christ in the 1820s in Copenhagen for the Cathedral Church of Our Lady.

This temple, commonly known as the Mesa Temple, was the seventh temple built by the growing church, and the first in Arizona. Construction began in 1922 and church leaders dedicated the Mesa Temple in 1927. In 1975, the temple was remodeled. Mormon temples are open for public tours prior to dedication, and the Mesa Temple was the first to conduct tours before a rededication. Although about 140,000 church members lived in Arizona at the time, 205,000 people toured the temple during the two-and-a-half-week period. The Mesa Temple was also the first temple to offer church ordinances in Spanish.

Location: Mesa, east of Phoenix.

Description: For all people of the Mormon faith, the temple represents the most sacred place on earth; the grounds, open to all, are serene and inviting.

How to get there: Go east on Loop 202 (Red Mountain Freeway) and exit south at Country Club Drive (Exit 13). Go about 3 miles and turn left (east) on Main Street. Go 1.25 miles. The Temple Visitors' Center, located in front of the temple, is on the south side of the street.

Friezes on the temple's exterior walls depict scenes of the Lord's people gathering in the Old World and the New World, in the Americas and on the Pacific Islands. Inside the temple, church members wear all-white clothing as a symbol of purity and equality before God. Mormon temples serve as the House of the Lord, where members receive in-depth teaching about the church. Baptism by full immersion occurs in temples as a central church teaching. Religious ceremonies are performed there on behalf of the living and the deceased, and marriages and families are sealed by the authority of the holy priesthood so that families may continue together throughout eternity. Members also trace genealogies and perform the ordinances in the name of ancestors so that those who died without hearing the church's message will have an opportunity to accept Christ and be joined with their families for all time.

During Christmas and Easter, the Mesa Temple hosts two of the largest seasonal activities in the world, and both are free. Every December, more than a million people come to see the Christmas display of 600,000-plus lights, which transform the grounds into a fairyland. Community choirs and church groups perform nightly concerts of sacred music. Camels made of lights march across the front lawn and a nearly life-size Nativity from Italy depicts Jesus' birth on a grand scale. No lights, however, hang from the temple because of its sacred nature.

At Easter, church members perform a musical/drama of Jesus' life called "Jesus the Christ" in the world's largest annual Passion play. The performances in English and Spanish portray Jesus' life from birth to crucifixion to resurrection. The pageant grew out of a small, sunrise Easter service in 1928. Today, performers use a state-of-the-art stage built specifically for the pageant, and costumes are as authentic as possible, thanks to careful research by church members. The Passion play draws such a crowd that, although 10,000 chairs fill the lawn in front of the visitors' center, each night of the performance is standing-room only.

18. Maha Ganapati Temple of Arizona

51933 W. Teel Rd.
Maricopa, AZ 85239
(480) 644-1252
www.ganapati.org

Mailing address:
P.O. Box 11368
Chandler, AZ 85248

*T*he beige modular building sits on 15 acres near Maricopa, past Harrah's Ak-Chin Casino and miles of farmland. Here, Arizona's growing Hindu community dreams of building the first temple in the state like the traditional stone temples of India, which have stood for more than 1,000 years. Such a temple here will bring a good vibration to Arizona, devotees say.

Devotees, some in business clothes, some in the traditional dress of India, arrive at the temple with food, flowers, and other offerings. What best translates in Western understanding as "God" gives everything, they believe, so you don't come to the temple empty-handed. You also are expected to remove your shoes before entering the temple, as you are walking on holy ground. The priest smudges ashes on the foreheads of devotees, a sign that humans return to ash, a reminder that tames the ego.

They pray in Sanskrit to the deity installed at the temple. In India and around the world, Hindus will go to any temple to worship, but temples do feature different deities, such as Vishnu or Shiva.

This temple centers on the son of Shiva, Lord Ganesha, the god who takes the form of an elephant and is the first focus of worship among most

Location: Maricopa, about 25 miles southwest of Chandler.

Description: Plans to become the first traditionally built, mainstream Hindu temple for all denominations and sects in Arizona; has an active membership.

How to get there: From the Phoenix area, take I-10 southeast toward Tucson. Exit on Queen Creek Road (Exit 164), which is AZ 347 South. After 3.5 miles, AZ 347 South turns into Maricopa Road. Drive for about 17 miles. Go west (right) on Papago Road for 5 miles, south (left) on Thunderbird Road for 2 miles, and east (left) on Teel Road for 0.5 mile. The temple's temporary structure is across the street from the vineyard on Teel Road and its mailing address is in Chandler.

devotees in India. The granite statue of the deity weighs about 1,400 pounds and hails from South India. One tusk is missing because Ganesha broke it to write the Vedas, the holy scripture. The deity has four arms, and in his left open palm lies sweet meat, symbolizing all the goodness he gives to the whole world. He has a rope to keep people from straying away from good deeds. He also has a mouse, symbolizing that no matter how large or small, if creatures are willing, they can carry holiness in them.

Hindus typically pray to Ganesha before they start any work. He is considered the "God of difficulties, God of roadblocks." Hindus call upon him to remove obstacles if their deeds are good and to put them in the way if their deeds are bad.

Hindus believe that the universe is made up of repeating cycles of creation, preservation, and destruction, and that humankind suffers from immaturity of the soul. They trust in the freedom to worship in a variety of ways and that all paths lead to God. Acts of worship center around both the temple and shrines installed in the home.

More than 500 members of the Hindu community came to Maha Ganapati Temple of Arizona's grand opening celebration in February 2002. Construction on the temple, to replace the 2,100-square-foot temporary building, is expected to start in 2003. They plan to turn the dusty acres into a community and cultural center for Arizona's Hindu population, as well as a place to worship. Maha Ganapati is the fourth Hindu temple in the Phoenix metropolitan area, but the others are housed in converted churches and a former martial arts building without as much property to expand.

Hindus do not proselytize, but they welcome visitors. To become a Hindu, you must live like a Hindu. The temple is open for services on weekends, some evenings, and on holidays. As the temple community grows, the services will expand. The temple employs a full-time spiritual leader from India who is trained in Rig Veda and temple rituals.

Retreats

19. Cave Creek Mistress Mine Healing & Retreat Center

P.O. Box 5754
Carefree, AZ 85377
(480) 488-0842
E-mail: ccmistress@aol.com
www.ccmistressmine.com

*T*ranquility, not gold, beckons modern-day visitors to Cave Creek Mistress Mine Healing & Retreat Center. The Tonto National Forest surrounds the 40 acres home to the historic Mistress Mine, first recorded as a gold mine in the 1880s, creating an escape far removed from the trappings of the city.

Location: Northeast of Carefree.

Description: An old gold mine turned into a rustic and remote retreat and healing center.

How to get there: From Loop 101, go north on Cave Creek Road (Exit 28) for about 40 minutes, following the signs for Seven Springs. Note that from Loop 101 to the Tonto National Forest entrance, it's about 22 miles, and Cave Creek Road turns into Forest Road 24 as it crosses the forest boundary. When the pavement ends, go another 1.6 miles. Look for the sign on the left and go up the hill, following a steep, dirt road (most sedans can make the trip).

The rock shop, mining museum, and gold panning here are fun diversions. But the real attractions at this out-of-the-way spot are opportunities such as spending the night in a teepee, participating in a meditation program led by Native American shamans, trying out a sweat lodge, or simply finding solitude on a search for spiritual peace. The director and caretaker of the mine, Ron Kaczor, has a master's degree in counseling and an affinity for the Native American spirituality that he shares. Wellness treatments also dip into New Age and Far East traditions with aura cleansing, aromatherapy, Chinese herbology, and more.

The hills, one side harsh and rocky and the other side green, lush, and fertile, create a place of balance. This integration of male and female heals, and you can feel the power of Mother Earth. The elevation, 3,700 feet, bestows the area with cooler summer days than the scorchers of the Valley floor.

Overnight guests best experience the full range of the place. The hot tub bubbles under starry skies and a massage table beckons under the leafy canopy of trees. Old mining equipment and rustic buildings on the property add character. A 1,000-year-old abandoned Hohokam village, the Sears-Kay Ruin, awaits exploration nearby. Accommodations in the retreat center's clean, one-room cabin are $35 per person per night and the teepee is $30. Rustic group accommodations at $15 to $20 per person per night consist of a bunkhouse and the second floor of another building, to which guests should bring a sleeping bag.

Hours for daytime visitors are 10 a.m. to 6 p.m. daily. The healing center accommodates small overnight groups as well as individuals, but not children. Massage, herbal wraps, astrology readings, and a variety of seminars fill the schedule of events offered here. This is not a resort, but rather a place to discover your inner peace.

20. Spirit in the Desert Lutheran Retreat Center

7415 E. Elbow Bend Rd.
Carefree, AZ 85377
(480) 488-5218
E-mail: sitdlrc@aol.com
www.spiritinthedesert.org

"Come away in the desert to a quiet place and rest a while," Jesus says in Mark 6:31. If taking time away for spiritual growth appeals to you, but the bare-bones amenities of many retreat centers do not, then you will find the perfect escape at Spirit in the Desert.

The retreat center started as the Adobe Inn, one of many lovely high-desert tourist destinations in the posh Carefree area, known for its upscale resorts and relaxed lifestyle. A national diet company later converted it into its corporate retreat center. Finally, in 1992, Malcolm Estrem—wealthy inventor of "the world's best hot chocolate machine," a fixture in nearly every Denny's and McDonald's across the globe—purchased the property as a gift to the Grand Canyon Synod of the Evangelical Lutheran Church in America.

Estrem had experienced significant spiritual growth at a retreat center in the Midwest, and he wanted to provide Arizonans with the same opportunities. He lived modestly and hoped to bless others the way the Lord blessed him. He succeeded by creating a lasting legacy of peace for the entire church. He lived to see his dream become reality at the dedication of Spirit in the Desert Lutheran Retreat Center. A second donation from the family went toward building a two-story addition and expanding the site to 6 acres.

Offering extras such as a heated swimming pool and proximity to shopping at Ho and Hum streets, Arizona's only Lutheran retreat center combines a retreat experience with all the creature comforts you'd want on a vacation. Private balconies with mountain views wrap around the buildings. The large guest rooms in the main conference center boast a fireplace, mini-refrigerator, wet bar, and private bath. In the 12-bedroom addition, a separate living room area connects to each pair of bedrooms. The retreat center's amenities for conferences include state-of-the-art meeting rooms with high-speed Internet access and real-time conferencing capabilities. A chef cooks all the meals and the property is wheelchair accessible.

But despite the resort-style facility, spirituality—rather than the mood of tourists on holiday—permeates the grounds. Spirit in the Desert's mission statement describes the center as "a place and time set apart for spiritual discovery, growth, and renewal." The setting allows for withdrawal from daily life—a chance to feel the presence of God's spirit move and to experience the creator's goodness.

Location: Carefree, north of Phoenix.
Description: Arizona's only Lutheran retreat center, located in a quiet desert community.
How to get there: From Loop 101, go north on Scottsdale Road (Exit 34) past Carefree Highway, where the road becomes North Tom Darlington Drive. Go 1.6 miles on North Tom Darlington Drive. Turn right (east) on Bloody Basin Road and go a short distance before turning left (north) on North Sidewinder Road. North Sidewinder Road curves into East Elbow Bend Road.

The surroundings celebrate the power of creation and beauty in nature. Instead of a bank of stained-glass windows in the chapel, large picture windows frame the mountains. For his Eagle Scout project, a local teenager built a labyrinth of natural stone on the property. The labyrinth symbolizes the pilgrimage to Jerusalem and the journey to a deeper relationship with God.

The retreat center draws Lutherans and non-Lutherans from around the world. One woman from Germany comes almost every year, for two weeks to two months, to the place where she says she "lost her heart and found her spirit." In Chicago, employees at the church's denominational offices make their retreat plans when the chilly Midwestern winds begin to blow.

Spirit in the Desert welcomes the solitary retreatant, the small group retreat, and the large retreat or conference. Single occupancy starts at $75 per night, not including meals. Reserving large rooms, with a combination of queen, full, and twin beds, lowers the per person rate. This arrangement perfectly suits a small group Bible study or family. Another way to save is by signing up for a package that combines accommodations with educational programs. The retreat center offers classes and spiritual direction, but allows groups to provide their own programs if they choose.

The sleeping rooms have no phones, but the front desk posts messages on a board in the lobby. Emergency messages are delivered immediately so those who feel uncomfortable completely disconnecting from the world will know they won't miss anything important.

Plan ahead for your stay. Current capacity is less than 100 people, and every year, more retreatants flock to the center. The most popular times to visit are January through May, but summer temperatures here hover 5 to 10 degrees below those of the Valley floor, making it a fine escape during the warmer months as well.

Spirit in the Desert is an independent ministry affiliated with the denomination and the synod. The center welcomes all faiths, although its mission is primarily to Christians of all denominations.

21. Franciscan Renewal Center

5802 E. Lincoln Dr.
Scottsdale, AZ 85253
(480) 948-7460
E-mail: casa@thecasa.org
www.thecasa.org

Rush-hour traffic renders Lincoln Drive a busy thoroughfare. Luxurious homes dot Mummy and Camelback mountains, part of the city growth that surrounds the property once so remote that Phoenicians of the time wondered why the Franciscans wanted to buy it. Still, the peace that drew the monks to this place nestled at the base of Camelback Mountain more than 50 years ago prevails at the Franciscan Renewal Center.

Ranchers no longer drive cattle across the property as they did in years past. Generous donations by those who found peace here allowed the friars to expand the center from one lodge for 44 people to a property encompassing 56 sleeping rooms with private baths, a swimming pool, and large and small meeting rooms. The center offers hundreds of organized programs, retreats, and classes each year.

Franciscan Renewal Center lives up to its familiar name, the Casa de Paz y Bien, Spanish for the "house of peace and good." Whether for an afternoon or a month, countless visitors find respite and renewal here, sans telephones, televisions, radios, and clocks.

The place bustles with activity, but its 23 acres allow more than enough space for solitude, even during the children's summer day camp program. Free from distraction, you can tread the quiet desert walkways as you reconnect, refocus, and grow spiritually. Inside the small chapel on the property, you can hear yourself breathe. (If the door is locked, ask for the key at the desk.) A labyrinth made of spiraling rocks beckons in the desert, and benches throughout the grounds provide shady or sunny spots to sit.

Jesus went away in the desert to pray, the fathers say, and all people, not just Catholics, will benefit from the spiritual and emotional rejuvenation

Location: Scottsdale, northeast of Phoenix.

Description: A Franciscan retreat center offering a wide variety of programs from yoga and step-parenting classes to solitary retreats.

How to get there: From AZ 51 (Squaw Peak Parkway) go east on Lincoln Drive (Exit 5). The retreat center is on the north side of Lincoln Drive, east of 56th Street.

that comes from following that example. The Franciscans live by the words of St. Francis of Assisi: "Preach the gospel. If necessary, use words." They believe that people are good, creation is good, and life is good. Their ministry embodies this creed through education, healing, hospitality, social action, and contemplative experience.

Since the 1980s, the Franciscan Renewal Center's reputation as a nonthreatening and gentle sanctuary has drawn those who struggle with faith, those who need a helping hand in their spiritual journey, those who are searching, and those who have felt alienated from the church and from the world. The friars welcome everyone, but the center is not interfaith: It's Catholic without apology, but no one pushes Catholicism on visitors. Christians of all kinds attend the programs and retreats, and non-Christians aren't required to attend Mass. If you go for a solitary retreat, you will be left alone.

The retreat center's founder, Father Owen da Silva, traveled to Phoenix from Malibu, Calif., to conduct retreats for Catholic laymen in the 1940s. As the retreat movement grew, he saw the need to find property here. Franciscan Renewal Center hosted the world's first group married couples' retreat in February 1952. All early retreats observed the strict rule of silence, even for married couples, an odd notion in today's climate of marriage retreats designed to improve communication skills. But those who attended the retreats said they were wonderful, and the silence gave them time for thinking.

Fewer retreats are silent today. And over the years, those early retreats for married couples changed into a time of reconnection for entire families. Parents and their children, grandchildren, and great-grandchildren now gather together for fun and worship with family and good friends.

Along with its numerous programs and group retreats, the center offers private spiritual direction and a diversity of counseling services. The counseling ministry here employs more than 20 professionals in private practice. Daily and weekend Mass take place at the center, which serves as a parish for those who attend regularly. The focus here is spirituality, but the fathers also foster a strong awareness of social justice and encourage involvement in volunteer activities.

22. Mt. Claret Retreat Center

4633 N. 54th St.
Phoenix, AZ 85018
(602) 840-5066

You forget that you're in the middle of one of the country's biggest cities when you frequent this serene enclave. Easygoing pathways of crushed granite, bordered by flowers and stones, lead up to benches before a large likeness of Our Lady of Guadalupe, the patroness of the Roman Catholic Diocese of Phoenix. Other benches scattered throughout the property invite only you and your own pensive thoughts.

If you want to escape the aggravations of urban life without having to travel outside the city limits, this is the place for you. You'll breathe in the scents of the desert and listen to the chirping of birds, rather than smelling the exhaust of rush-hour traffic and cringing at each impatient honk of the commuters' horns. The desert creates a buffer between the Mt. Claret property and surrounding houses, so you'll feel alone amidst the creosote bushes and Joshua trees.

Individuals are welcome to come for a private, self-directed stay at the well-kept retreat center, but space is limited and meals are not included. For most people, the desert garden makes for a lovely place to pray and meditate in front of Our Lady of Guadalupe, and to spend an hour or an afternoon in retreat from the metropolitan hustle. Admission to the garden and chapel is free; call ahead to check rates for overnight stays.

Location: Central Phoenix, near Camelback Mountain.
Description: A Catholic retreat center with a desert garden for peaceful prayer in the middle of the city.
How to get there: From I-17, go east on Camelback Road (Exit 203). Go left (north) on 54th Street. The road ends in the Mt. Claret Retreat Center parking lot.

23. Our Lady of Guadalupe Monastery

8502 W. Pinchot Ave.
Phoenix, AZ 85037
(623) 848-9608
E-mail: bensrs@aol.com
www.benedictinespirit.org

Location: West Phoenix.

Description: A Catholic monastery for the Sisters of St. Benedict, with peaceful surroundings inside and out; lends itself to a day of solitude or a retreat, either group or private.

How to get there: From I-10, go north on 83rd Avenue (Exit 135) for 1.2 miles. Turn left (west) on West Thomas Road. Go almost 0.5 mile, then go right (north) on North 86th Drive and into the neighborhood. Go right (east) on West Verde Lane, left (north) on North 86th Avenue, and right (east) on West Pinchot Avenue. The monastery is on the left behind the gates.

*I*n their previous lives as nursery grounds, these two acres nurtured the growth of flowers, plants, and trees. Now home to Our Lady of Guadalupe Monastery, this land today engenders faith.

The Sisters of St. Benedict founded the community in 1986 as the only place in Arizona where a nun can receive training for the vocation. The word "convent" is absent from its name because the Vatican decided that any monastic community, whether made up of males or females, should be called a monastery.

This monastery, dedicated in 1998, ranks as one of the nicest venues in the Valley for a day of solitude or a retreat. Tall bottlebrush trees shade the grounds. Cool, arched walkways surround the buildings. The 12 guest rooms, which vary in size to accommodate a single person or a group, are clean, pleasant, and cheerful.

The sisters offer directed retreats. If you seek solitude, they will pray for you, as a decorative notice in the bedroom proclaims: "We hope that your stay here will nourish your body and soul. We have been praying for you throughout this week."

The Southwestern design of the monastery and chapel bears Mexican and Native American influences. Stained-glass windows by renowned Southwestern artist Ted De Grazia filter the light in the saltillo-tiled chapel. The sisters pray the Liturgy of the Hours for the morning and evening prayers, and retreatants are invited to join them. A balcony above the chapel's main floor also makes a pleasant, more secluded place to pray.

More than 100 years old, the monastery's statue of St. Anthony belonged to the grandfather of the prioress. A grotto with Our Lady of Guadalupe is in the side yard.

Retreats are inexpensive. Private retreats are $35 a night per person, and meals are included. The retreat for Lent, including a two-night stay and all meals, costs $100 per person.

Unlike other monasteries, Benedictine communities are not considered "contemplative"—meaning the women here do not spend their days cloistered and in prayer. Work is prayer, they say.

One of the sisters runs a small day-care center at Our Lady of Guadalupe, making it likely one of few monasteries with a playground in the back yard. On weekdays, the monastery is most quiet during naptime, early in the morning, and in the evening. The wing with the retreat rooms is separate from the main part of the monastery, so the sounds of the children rarely spill over.

Our Lady of Guadalupe Monastery holds monthly meetings for women interested in monastic life. A woman need not give up an outside career to join the order, but she must be Roman Catholic, between the ages of 21 to 45, drawn to community, spiritual, active in her parish, and single and free to make vows.

The sisters follow the Rule of St. Benedict: "Seeking workers in a multitude of people, God calls out and says again: 'Is there anyone who yearns for life and desires to see good days?' God then directs these words to you: 'If you desire true and eternal life, keep your tongue free from vicious talk and your lips from all deceit; turn away from evil and do good; let peace be your quest and aim.'"

If peace is *your* quest and aim, you're likely to find it here.

24. Wat Promkunaram Buddhist Temple of Arizona

17212 W. Maryland Ave.
Waddell, AZ 85355
(623) 935-2276
E-mail: watprom@iirt.net

Chicks chase the mother hen. Dogs bark. An occasional jet from Luke Air Force Base roars overhead. On 5.5 acres in the midst of farmland, Thai Buddhist monks chant, teach, and practice their tenets.

Wat Promkunaram Buddhist Temple of Arizona held its grand opening in 1989. The temple serves the Thai Buddhist community along with Laotian, Cambodian, Vietnamese, and American Buddhists. The goal here is to promote peace, happiness, harmony, and love.

Buddhists believe that wisdom comes from within. You study the mind to pinpoint cravings and deficiencies. Through walking, sitting, and standing meditation exercises, you quiet the mind and focus on the body, on what you are doing at that moment. The

practice of meditation benefits the body's overall well-being by reducing stress, and it's one of the reasons that more people every year find their way to the temple and its retreats.

Location: Waddell, west of Phoenix.
Description: A Thai Buddhist temple offering retreats with a focus on meditation and the teachings of Buddha.
How to get there: From I-10, go north on Cotton Lane (Exit 124). Go left (west) on Maryland Avenue. The temple is a short distance on the right.

Each February, the monks hold an annual retreat—mostly silent—with walking, sitting, and standing meditation. Accommodations are modest at best, as men and women bring sleeping bags and spend the night on the floor in separate buildings. During the retreat, participants must follow several simple rules: They must refrain from killing any living being, stealing, lying, sexual misconduct, and intoxicants.

The English-language talks help you to understand the theoretical background for the Vipassana (insight) form of meditation, as well as the 2,500-year-old practices taught by Buddha. The monks do not charge for retreats, but it's customary to make a donation. The community takes care of the monks and that is considered good merit.

The monks also take in serious students who want to explore Buddhist teachings in depth. The temple holds regular weekend services, special holiday celebrations, and classes on Thai language, dance, and classical music. Operating hours at the temple are typically 8:30 a.m. to 8:30 p.m., and you are expected to remove your shoes before entering the sala, the main building where the monks live and the Buddhist rites take place.

Day-to-day life at the Thai Buddhist temple focuses on its present spiritual activities, not on its past as the site of one of the state's worst massacres. On August 10, 1991, two teenagers broke into the temple and killed nine people, including six Buddhist monks. A judge sentenced the perpetrators to nearly 300 years each in prison. A monument on the property pays homage to the memory of the victims.

You can't change the past, one of the practitioners says, but you can focus on today and influence the future with proper behavior.

25. Haku-un-ji Zen Center

1448 E. Cedar St.
Tempe, AZ 85281
(480) 894-6353
E-mail: sokai@zenarizona.com
www.zenarizona.com

Zen practitioners meditate silently long before the chattering birds wake this quiet residential neighborhood at dawn. Mature trees shade the large, lush back yard that smells of fresh earth, flowers, and newly cut grass. In the ivy under the trees, the statue of Jizo stands guard. He's found along roads in Japan, where he is venerated as the helper and protector of travelers. One Buddha sits in a fountain—not a traditional setting, laughs Sokai Geoffrey Barratt, the center's priest in residence. But it is Arizona and it is hot in the summer. A spare zendo, the building for meditation and educational talks, completes this Zen sanctuary in the desert, perfect for both the longtime Buddhist practitioner and the beginner.

Location: Tempe, east of Phoenix.
Description: A Zen Buddhist retreat center affiliated with Rinzai-ji Zen centers across the United States.
How to get there: From Loop 202 (Red Mountain Freeway), go south on McClintock Drive (Exit 8). Go 2 miles and turn right (west) on Apache Boulevard. Drive 0.25 mile and turn left (south) on Elm Street. Go left (east) on Cedar Street, the third street. The center is in a home on the north side of the street.

The low, resonant knock of a mallet against the "han" marks time here, not an alarm clock. The han, a wooden block bearing Japanese calligraphy, hangs on the back porch. Its symbol means, "It is the mind of the Buddha," and it's struck traditionally at dawn, when there's enough light to see the lines on the palm of your hand.

Few retreat centers locate in the Valley because the cooler temperatures in northern Arizona make that part of the state more attractive for church camps and spiritual retreats. But, for this Zen center, Sokai wanted to establish a respite without a three-hour drive from the metropolitan area. The priest chose the established neighborhood near Arizona State University for its location, solitude, and peaceful ambience. And the mature trees in the nearly quarter-acre back yard, along with covered patios and benches, provide a cool retreat even in the throes of summer.

The local community of Zen practitioners meets here for meditation and study. Although the practitioners meditate at home as well, the center provides an escape in the city, free of work and life distractions. The center also offers numerous retreats throughout the year, from one day to several days in length. It advertises little, yet retreats always fill up and every week someone new comes by.

Haku-un-ji Zen Center founding priest Sokai, an American, studied with Zen master Kyozan Joshu Roshi for more than 10 years before settling in Arizona. Roshi, along with his students, has overseen the establishment of more than a dozen Rinzai-ji Zen centers throughout the United States since arriving here in 1962 from Japan. Haku-un-ji Zen Center opened in 1994 as an affiliate of the main temple in Los Angeles. Although in his 90s, Roshi visits the Tempe center twice a year to lead retreats; Sokai conducts weekly sessions and other retreats.

Roshi teaches the rigorous discipline of Rinzai Zen. Zen is the largest school of Buddhism in Japan, and although it's spreading, he says, Buddhism puzzles many Americans who struggle with the idea of a spiritual practice without God at its core. Meditation and all activities center on the present moment rather than the future or past. Sitting meditation focuses on breathing and letting all thoughts disappear, revealing the true self in this state of emptiness. At that point, God does not exist as an object because the person experiences God in the perfect self. The practice leads to the understanding of the fundamental, unfixed nature of the self and the universe.

Roshi and his disciples make the exploration and study of Zen accessible to Americans who live and work in a multitasking, rapid-fire world. Retreats vary, but simplicity and discipline set the tone. The house accommodates small groups of guests in basic bedrooms or in sleeping bags on the floor. Retreatants rise as early as 3:30 a.m., and bedtime comes as soon as 8:30 p.m. The group practices sitting and walking meditation, silence, and chanting during this time set aside to focus only on the spiritual.

Retreats range in size from 20 to 50 guests and space fills up quickly. A one-day retreat starts at $25 and a three-day retreat starts at $150, meals included. Membership to the center costs $20 a month and includes a newsletter and discounts on retreats. Sokai turns no one away from a retreat for inability to pay: He works out alternate arrangements for the serious student, which might involve volunteering at the center.

Sacred Places

26. Deer Valley Rock Art Center

3711 W. Deer Valley Rd.
Phoenix, AZ 85080
(623) 582-8007
E-mail: dvrac@asu.edu
www.asu.edu/clas/anthropology/dvrac/

*R*ock- and cactus-covered mountains created millions of years ago by volcanic eruption fill the landscape of the northwest Valley. More than 1,500 petroglyphs cover the east side of the Hedgpeth Hills, distinguishing them from other mountains in the area.

Native Americans view this site the same way Catholics view a cathedral. Just as the stained-glass windows of the old cathedrals tell the story of the Christian faith, the petroglyph site connects Native Americans to the past through a written history.

Testing has dated the petroglyphs from between 9400–6500 B.C. and A.D. 1225. The most unusual panel is a mirror image of a deer that looks like two of the animals kissing. Archaeologists have found nothing like it at other petroglyph sites in the state.

Deciphering the precise meaning of petroglyphs remains puzzling today because the ancient cultures that created them no longer exist. But descendents give insight: Some petroglyphs represent the journey of the soul, and Yavapai people have recognized such designs at Deer Valley. The animals could symbolize hunting magic or clan identification, as Hopi elders have identified clan markings here. According to the interpretations in the visitors' center, they could be messages left to others for purposes of indicating the place's sacred nature, curing sickness, and maintaining cosmological order.

Location: About 30 minutes northwest of Phoenix.

Description: A connection with the ancient past and modern spirituality of Native Americans.

How to get there: From I-17, go north to Deer Valley Road (Exit 217B) and go west about 2.5 miles. Bear right at the fork in the road and head into the parking lot at the dead end. The center is west of 35th Avenue and its location is well signed.

The Hedgpeth Hills face east, but no patterns emerge during equinoxes or solstices as at some petroglyph sites. Perhaps the site corresponded with a major trade route. The Hohokam did live in the area from A.D. 900 to 1150, although they did not build homes on this mountain.

To make the petroglyphs, the ancient artists pecked away at the dark "rock varnish" covering the boulders. The desert's infamous dust storms blanketed the boulders with dirt, which reacted with bacteria on the rock surface and sunlight to create the patina so perfect for chiseling.

The crushed gravel, 0.25-mile path is easy to walk and is wheelchair accessible. Many petroglyphs are close to the path. Viewing tubes help you to find particular petroglyphs situated higher on the mountain, but binoculars enhance careful study so you might want to pack some.

Please show respect for this and other such sacred places by never touching petroglyphs or making rubbings or casts of them. The oils on your hands and the pressure of invasive copying methods compromise the fragile markings. At the Deer Valley center, please keep to the path. Climbing on the rocks damages the petroglyphs (and rattlesnakes hang out on the mountain).

Arizona State University's Department of Anthropology manages the site, listed on both the National Register of Historic Places and the Phoenix Historic Property Register. Phoenicians discovered the site in the 1930s while building a dam and decided to preserve the rare find. In 1994, the Deer Valley Rock Art Center opened to educate the public about petroglyphs.

Inside a low-slung building that blends well with its surroundings, interesting displays for adults and children make a good start for your tour. In the summer, early mornings provide the most solitude for sitting on the benches and pondering these markings. Changing light throughout the day renders some panels easier to see. Hours of operation vary, so call first. The entry fee per person is low and an annual membership is affordable.

The center offers a variety of classes, field trips, and programs, held here and at other petroglyph sites in the Valley. The Pueblo Grande Museum in Phoenix also conducts guided hikes at different petroglyph sites. Call (602) 495-0900 for more information.

27. Gardens at the COFCO Chinese Cultural Center

668 N. 44th St.
Phoenix, AZ 85008
(602) 275-8578
E-mail: info@cofcochineseculturalcr.com
www.cofcochineseculturalcr.com

*I*n a sea of stucco houses with tiled roofs, the Chinese Cultural Center stands out as a wonderful architectural anomaly in the Valley of the Sun. Within the yellow-roofed rows of shops and restaurants, the Asian community re-created five traditional Chinese gardens punctuated by replicas of ancient pagodas and statuary.

Acclaimed designer Madame Yi employed the principles of feng shui to produce in these gardens a harmonious environment. The gardens' designs create optimal conditions for enabling the flow of chi, an invisible energy that moves freely. But depending on the arrangement of the surroundings, chi can become trapped, with too little or too much building up in one space. Through balancing yin and yang, the light and dark, the perfect flow of chi—and thus, balance—is achieved. When the chi flows appropriately, good fortune and positive energy increase.

Plaques throughout explain the symbolism and beliefs surrounding these large gardens, a good place to sit alone and meditate or to learn more about Chinese culture. Open daily from 7 a.m. to 7 p.m. Admission is free.

Location: East Phoenix, near Phoenix Sky Harbor International Airport.
Description: A cultural, culinary, and retail center featuring replicas of five traditional Chinese gardens.
How to get there: From Loop 202 (Red Mountain Freeway), go south at 40th/44th Street (Exit 2). The gardens are connected to the Chinese Cultural Center on 44th Street.

28. Sears-Kay Ruin and the Tonto National Forest

Main Ranger Office
2324 E. McDowell Rd.
Phoenix, AZ 85006
(602) 225-5200
www.fs.fed.us/r3/tonto

The Tonto National Forest begins near the northern and eastern edges of metropolitan Phoenix and stretches to the piney high country. The elevation ranges from 1,300 feet to almost 8,000 feet.

In the desert of the Tonto National Forest exist numerous abandoned Hohokam villages, more than 900 years old, along with evidence of other cultures. One of the best preserved and most accessible is Sears-Kay Ruin, the remains of a 40-room pueblo. The Hohokam who lived here had views

Location: Northeast of metropolitan Phoenix.

Description: Three million acres of desert merging into pines, with numerous prehistoric archaeological sites; a site of note near the metro area is the Sears-Kay Ruin.

How to get there: For specific trail information, it's best to start with the ranger office, which offers detailed maps of hiking trails and campsites. To get to Sears-Kay Ruin from Loop 101, go north on Cave Creek Road (Exit 28)— which turns into Forest Road 24 at the entrance to the national forest—for 23 miles. At the sign for Sears-Kay, turn right and continue for 0.3 mile to the parking lot and trailhead.

of the row of mountains called Four Peaks, as well as of Weaver's Needle, a mountain that juts up from the desert floor in the shape of its namesake.

In his book *11,000 Years on Tonto National Forest*, archaeologist J. Scott Wood explains, "The Hohokam tradition dominated cultural growth in much of central Arizona for close to 1,200 years." The settlements developed from simple farming villages to a more complex city structure with sophisticated irrigation canal systems and trade routes. These villages and the mountains that cradle them are sacred because of their connection to the past, though much about the settlements remains a mystery.

Open during the day, the trail is a short, steep hike; signs along the way explain the site's significance. Bring your own water, wear hiking boots or comfortable walking shoes, and watch for rattlesnakes. No fee is required to enter the site, and you'll find no facilities there except picnic tables and a toilet. Please respect the integrity of the site by leaving it as you found it.

The ranger district schedules the occasional guided tour, which is free. But here, alone in an undeveloped part of the desert without a visitors' center, you can really connect with the past in silence as you ponder the fate of centuries.

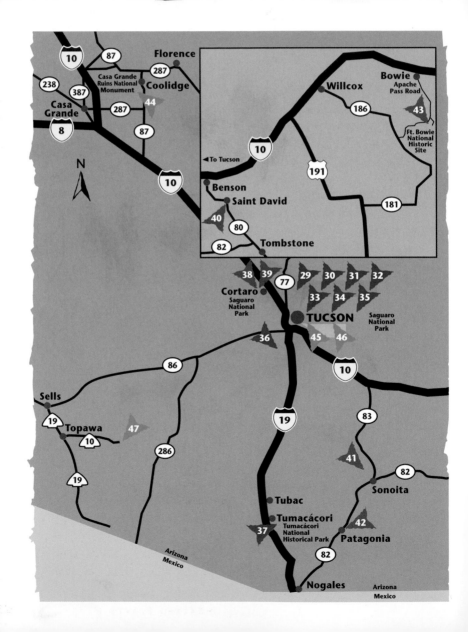

$\mathcal{T}$he influences of Native Americans and early Spanish missionaries define modern-day Tucson and southern Arizona. The spirit of the ancient Hohokam still courses through Casa Grande, the largest existing structure built by these native peoples and the first archaeological preserve designated by the U.S. government. The area's heritage also includes the historic missions of San Xavier del Bac and San José de Tumacácori. Their origins predate the writing of the Declaration of Independence, though Franciscan priests and Native American tribes did not construct the mission churches until the 18th and 19th centuries.

Tucson is the state's second-largest city, whereas the rest of southern Arizona consists of sparsely populated ranches, Indian reservations, mountains, and wide-open desert. Tucked between the peaks

and the cactus, Tucson is not a city in a desert so much as a desert that has made room for a city. Within Tucson exist tributes to God and nature, evident in the Mission in the Sun chapel, built by celebrated Southwestern artist Ted De Grazia and his Native American friends, and Sunrise Chapel, designed to frame the surrounding mountains.

On Tucson's edges you'll find wonderful retreat centers, easily accessible but with night skies so dark, you could spend the rest of your life simply counting the multitudes of stars. And deep in southern Arizona, undisturbed solitude awaits far from the city: Witness destinations such as Holy Trinity Monastery, noted for its 70-foot-tall Celtic cross, and Tree of Life Rejuvenation Center, an eco-healing retreat designed to bring body, mind, and spirit into balance.

Sanctuaries

29. Mission in the Sun

6300 N. Swan Rd.
Tucson, AZ 85718
(520) 299-9191
E-mail: gallerysun@aol.com
www.degrazia.org

*B*efore Ted De Grazia constructed a gallery for his distinctive artwork, he hand-built a chapel for Christians, non-Christians, and the spiritually curious. Set against a backdrop of mountains and lush desert, Mission in the Sun—a small, stone-floored, adobe chapel with a few rough wooden benches—lifts your spirit as it pays homage to faith, loveliness, and simplicity.

With the help of some Native American friends, De Grazia built the chapel in 1953 to honor missionary Padre Kino and dedicated it to Our Lady of Guadalupe, the virgin saint of Mexico who appeared to Juan Diego in 1531. The interior comes alive with De Grazia murals, well executed in his colorful style that celebrates Native American and Southwest cultures. Painted angels dance along one wall. Sunshine pours through the roof's open slats, and the thick adobe walls keep the chapel cool, even on warm days.

The altar overflows with pictures of so many lost ones, mementos of children who died, a tiny stuffed bunny, seashells, crosses, and a baseball inscribed with the words, "I love you, bro." Happier memories live here, as well. The chapel is popular for small weddings, yet lends itself equally to quiet, private moments for prayer.

De Grazia's work incorporates many religious themes, evident in the oil and watercolor paintings, enamels, ceramics, jewelry, and other pieces displayed in the sprawling, hacienda-style gallery, which contains the largest and most complete collection of his work in existence. Some rooms have permanent displays and others rotate the artwork. A bronze fountain with a Yaqui deer dancer and a marvelous painting of Our Lady of Guadalupe anchor the gallery's inner courtyard. Wooden benches are scattered throughout, making this a wonderful outside spot to sit and think.

The gallery is open from 10 a.m. to 4 p.m., and admission is free. The chapel is open during daylight hours.

Location: East Tucson.
Description: An intimate chapel in the desert built and decorated by artist Ted De Grazia.
How to get there: From I-10, take Ina Road (Exit 248) east for about 7 miles. Go right (southeast) on Skyline Drive and continue for about 4 miles. At Swan Road, turn right (south). The chapel and gallery are a short distance on the left (east) side of the road.

30. Sunrise Chapel

8421 E. Wrightstown Rd.
Tucson, AZ 85715
(520) 298-1245
E-mail: sunchapel@aol.com
http://aztec.asu.edu/worship/sunrise/

*I*n some churches, the sight of gorgeous stained-glass windows takes your breath away. At Sunrise Chapel, the grand windows on the north side perfectly frame the Santa Catalina Mountains, showing off God's creation in a breathtaking natural view.

Behind a massive, uncut stone that serves as the altar, arched windows showcase Agua Caliente Hill, the Rincon Mountains, and a large cactus. The altar, made of banded gneiss, contains probably about $100 worth of gold. Removing the gold would cost much more than that, but the church members and the Rev. Frank Rose nevertheless prefer to keep the gold embedded in the rock as God made it. Rose, the church's pastor, says that no matter how beautiful, manmade objects might lose their power of inspiration over time, but God's creation never does.

An open Bible perches on the stone altar. The sun shines on the Bible every day at 11 a.m., no matter what time of the year. A crystal hangs over the Bible, splashing rainbows around the room.

On the south wall of the chapel hang three-dimensional sculptures of two mountains. These works of papier-mâché and paint depict Mount Sinai, where Moses received the Ten Commandments, and the Mount of Olives, where Jesus prayed and from where he ascended into heaven.

The chapel, part of the General Church of the New Jerusalem, follows the teachings of Emanuel Swedenborg (1688–1772). The Swedish scientist and theologian wrote extensively about the Bible in an effort to detail the Lord's plan for a new era of Christianity and religious understanding. The church holds that all religions have value and that God draws people through whatever religious convictions they have. The teachings focus on the spiritual meaning of the Bible, with an emphasis on the spiritual journey. Sunrise Chapel's surroundings enhance that experience with its light, open design and mountain scenery.

Location: East Tucson.
Description: A Christian chapel built to celebrate the beauty of nature.
How to get there: From I-10, take Speedway Boulevard (Exit 257) east for about 9 miles. Go left (north) on Pantano Road for 1 mile. Go right (east) on Wrightstown Road and continue for about 0.75 mile. The chapel is on the north side of Wrightstown Road, between Pantano Road and Camino Seco.

The congregation has called Tucson home since the 1950s. Sunrise Chapel was dedicated in 1987 to allow the congregation room to grow. In designing the chapel, they wanted to create a space that honored the beauty of nature—a space that, according to the pastor, now moves some people to tears when they first enter.

The chapel is popular for weddings and couples are encouraged to design their own service. Couples do not have to join the congregation to be married there. The chapel accommodates 150 people comfortably. The children's chapel, a special meeting place for the younger set, has stained-glass windows, including one with Jesus blessing children of all races.

Sunrise Chapel's Sunday services take place at 11 a.m., and various classes and groups convene here throughout the week. Sunrise Chapel is open weekdays from 9 a.m. to 4 p.m. An outdoor meditation path, the Path of Faith, is always open for exploration.

31. Islamic Center of Tucson

901 E. First St.
Tucson, AZ 85719
(520) 624-3233
www.ictucson.com

A brick and stucco building topped with two domes and a crescent, the Islamic Center of Tucson (ICT) sits on the edge of the University of Arizona campus. Offering religious, cultural, social, and educational programs, it serves as the center of spiritual and community life for Muslim students and the Tucson metro area's Muslim population.

Location: Tucson, near the University of Arizona campus.
Description: A multicultural mosque with outreach programs for students.
How to get there: From I-10, go east on Speedway Boulevard (Exit 257). Turn right (south) on Tyndall Avenue. The mosque is on the northeast corner of Tyndall Avenue and First Street.

University students established the mosque in 1966 as a means of gathering and praying with other Muslims. Without headquarters, they met at private houses or reserved rooms on the campus for their activities. In 1976, the group opened its first mosque near the campus. In the 1980s, membership increased as more Muslims came from around the world to study at the university. So, at a cost of about $1 million, the organization built the current mosque to accommodate the growth.

The ICT houses an Islamic school for children ages 5 to 13. It's also home to the Muslim Student Association, an organization that strengthens friendships among members and promotes good relations between Muslims and non-Muslims, who are free to join as associate members. Along with putting together religious and social activities, the association helps new students adjust to campus life, provides free tutoring to Muslim students, and publishes a weekly newsletter.

Muslims believe that about 1,400 years ago, God revealed the Koran to Mohammed, the last prophet of God. They worship the same God of Christianity and Judaism, whom they call Allah because Arabic is the common language of Islam. They believe in five major tenets, or pillars, of faith: They worship one God, pray five times a day facing Mecca, fast during the holy month of Ramadan, give to the poor, and make a pilgrimage to Mecca once in a lifetime, if physically able.

Everyone removes their shoes before entering a mosque, and women, even non-Muslims, are asked to cover their heads with scarves as a sign of modesty. Events and times of prayer change at the ICT, depending on the time of year. For information on Friday prayer services and other activities, call the mosque.

32. Little Chapel of All Nations

1401 E. First St.
Tucson, AZ 85719
(520) 623-1692

Mailing address:
P.O. Box 40995
Tucson, AZ 85719

The bright aqua door stands out on the quiet side street near fraternity and sorority houses at the busy University of Arizona. "Peace on Earth" and an image of a dove are etched into the glass arch over the door, a sign of the calm respite that awaits you inside.

Behind the small altar for kneeling, a large mural of the Earth commands attention on the chapel's back wall. The words painted below the mural are an updated rendition of those penned by poet Archibald MacLeish upon seeing the famous "Earthrise" photo taken from beyond the moon in 1968. The message defines the chapel's mission and offers food for contemplation:

> To see the Earth as it truly is, small and blue and beautiful in that eternal silence where it floats, is to see ourselves as riders on the Earth together, riders on that bright loveliness in the eternal cold and riders who know now they are truly brothers and sisters.

Location: Tucson, on the University of Arizona campus.

Description: A small chapel dedicated to all faiths.

How to get there: From I-10, take Speedway Boulevard (Exit 257) east about 4 miles. Go right (south) on Cherry. At First Street, turn right (west) and continue for one-and-a-half blocks. The chapel entrance is on your right, and the parking lot is on the east side of the building.

Ada Peirce McCormick, a wealthy social activist from the East Coast whose husband taught at the university, started the campus chapel in 1936 as a place for all people to feel welcome. The chapel has had several names over the years, but in 1954 it was incorporated as the Little Chapel of All Nations.

The original chapel was in an adobe house. When repair efforts became too expensive, the house was torn down to make way for the current structure, built in 1990. Along with the intimate chapel, which seats about 25, the building includes offices and a large library with books from Ada Peirce McCormick's private collection. Religious organizations such as Protestant and Buddhist groups also use the building.

The chapel is a popular campus spot for weddings, renewals of vows, baptisms, memorial services, and classes. Chapel hours are 8 a.m. to 5 p.m., Monday through Friday, although other times can be scheduled.

33. Bodhisattva Institute

714 N. Desert Ave.
Tucson, AZ 85711
(520) 325-2272

A "bodhisattva" is someone who has reached a high level of realization and is committed only to activities that benefit all beings. The decade-old Bodhisattva Institute, a center for the study and practice of Tibetan Buddhism, helps the devoted to follow that path.

Located in a residential neighborhood, the institute maintains a regular schedule of Tibetan chanting, mantra recitation, and meditation. Traditional paintings, ceremonial objects, flowers, incense, and candles fill the shrine room, which accommodates about 20 people comfortably. The group rents other venues for larger programs.

The institute follows the tradition of the Dakpo and Shangpa Kagyu lineages. It is affiliated with the Kagyu Droden Kunchab Center for the Study and Practice of Mahayana and Vajrayana Buddhism in San Francisco, under the spiritual direction of Lama Lodu Rinpoche. He visits the Tucson facility at least once a year for special teachings; the resident teacher is Lama Jinpa Tharchin.

Location: East Tucson.
Description: A center for the study and practice of Tibetan Buddhism.
How to get there: From I-10, go east on Speedway Boulevard (Exit 257). Go right (south) on Swan Road for 0.5 mile. Go right (west) on Fifth Street for a few blocks, then turn right (north) on Desert Avenue. The institute is on the right. Park on Fourth Street or Third Street.

Many people wonder how to get started with Buddhist meditation. You sit down and remain quiet, without letting your mind stray a million miles away or fill with worry. Calm-abiding meditation is a deliberate practice, working on your mind in the same way you exercise to strengthen your muscles. As you achieve more control, you see changes in your own behavior. Your patience grows as you move toward the ultimate goal of compassion and wisdom to benefit all beings. Though you might first enter the door of the shrine room to step away from the world, the more you learn, the more you realize this practice will motivate you to help others.

The practice schedule is Mahakala at 6:30 p.m., Monday through Saturday, followed by Chenrezig at 7 p.m. Mahakala is a practice specifically for students who have received the initiation from a teacher, but everyone is welcome to come for the blessing at the end. Chenrezig cultivates loving kindness and compassion, and anyone may participate in this hour-long practice. On Sunday mornings, Shamata, calm-abiding meditation, takes place at 9 a.m., followed by Chenrezig.

34. Temple Emanu-El

225 N. Country Club Rd.
Tucson, AZ 85716
(520) 327-4501
E-mail: temple@templeemanueltucson.org
www.templeemanueltucson.org

Thirteen members of Tucson's Jewish community met in 1910 to officially organize the Hebrew Benevolent Society, the first Jewish congregation in the Arizona territory. After five years of fund raising, that year the congregation settled into its original facility on Stone Avenue, the state's first Jewish house of worship and Tucson's oldest Reform Jewish synagogue. Women played an instrumental part in raising funds to establish the synagogue, built at a cost of $4,712.

Location: East Tucson.
Description: The oldest Jewish congregation in Arizona.
How to get there: From I-10, take Congress Street east (Exit 258). After about 1 mile, Congress turns into Broadway Boulevard. Continue east for 1 more mile, then turn left (north) on Country Club Road. The synagogue is on the left (west) side of the road.

The first services took place there on the eve of Rosh Hashanah, October 3, 1910, as the congregation celebrated the Jewish New Year and the start of the High Holy Days. The congregation, which changed its name to Temple Emanu-El, grew in its original location until 1949, when it moved to its current site. Between 1949 and 1962, the congregation augmented the facility with a multipurpose auditorium, offices, classrooms, and the sanctuary.

Programs are available for people of all ages. The synagogue houses a preschool for children 6 weeks to 5 years old, as well as religious school programs for elementary-age students through high-schoolers. In the educational programs, the goal is for the child to learn the joy and beauty of Judaism in a fun environment. The programs also prepare young boys and girls for their bar mitzvah or bat mitzvah, the rite-of-passage ceremony that signifies their entries into the community as adults.

The congregation reaches out to the community in many ways, including participation in Operation Deep Freeze, during which homeless people are provided shelter in the winter. Hours of operation and services vary at the temple, so call ahead for times.

35. Benedictine Sanctuary of Perpetual Adoration

800 N. Country Club Rd.
Tucson, AZ 85716
(520) 325-6401
www.benedictinesisters.org

*I*nside the beautiful, rose-colored church, Benedictine sisters practice the mystery of their Roman Catholic faith. From the moment they arrived in Tucson in 1935, the sisters have kept a 24-hour prayer vigil, praying for peace and reconciliation in the world. They pray before the Blessed Sacrament—the communion wafer that during the Eucharist, through the power of God, becomes the real presence of Jesus. The sisters seek to go beyond prayer and become perpetual adorers of Christ, to see him in everything.

Such constant meditation in the presence of Jesus has created a power that draws people from outside the monastic community to this quiet, peaceful place. Although the sisters do not have an official parish, many people join them for Sunday Mass and to pray for peace before the Blessed Sacrament. One sister explains that people keep coming here although they sometimes aren't sure why. She knows. It's the presence of Christ.

Location: East Tucson.
Description: A community of Benedictine sisters who invite others to join them for prayer and worship.
How to get there: From I-10, go east on Speedway Boulevard (Exit 257) for about 3 miles. Go right (south) on Country Club Road; the monastery will be on your right after 0.25 mile.

The sisters are part of the Congregation of the Benedictine Sisters of Perpetual Adoration. The order's 130 members live in four monasteries throughout the United States. They came to Tucson at the request of Bishop Daniel Gercke, who wanted to establish a community dedicated to prayer. Because some within their community suffered from tuberculosis, the sisters welcomed the invitation to settle in arid Arizona.

Upon construction in 1940, the Spanish Renaissance-style church and monastery earned the nickname the "pink rose of the desert." The chapel was built and consecrated in 1955. Nothing but open land surrounded the church. The sisters of those days did not drive, so faithful Catholics would bring them groceries and take care of their needs.

Then, the sisters earned money by growing oranges and dates. One advertising brochure posed the question, "Do nuns have dates?" Inside, it answered, "Yes, in the Friendship Garden."

Today, the sisters sew such items as liturgical vestments and altar linens, publish *Spirit & Life* magazine, and answer letters from people around the world who turn to them for spiritual guidance. They pray for all those who share their lives and problems through their letters. Prayer is their most important work.

Although surrounded by busy streets, the chapel is a serene and holy place to spend time with God. The chapel is open Sunday through Friday from 6:30 a.m. until the last service. On Saturday, the chapel opens at 6 a.m. Visiting priests say Sunday Mass. A contemplative prayer group meets on Monday nights, and the Days of Intensive Prayer offer further opportunities for spiritual exploration.

36. Mission San Xavier del Bac

1950 W. San Xavier Rd.
Tucson, AZ 85746
(520) 294-2624

*I*n Arizona, where often the new is more celebrated than the old, Mission San Xavier del Bac perseveres in beauty and grace. Father Eusebio Kino, a Jesuit missionary who established churches in Arizona and Mexico, founded the congregation in 1692. But construction on what would become the gleaming "White Dove of the Desert" did not begin until the 18th century.

Various priests and Native Americans in southern Arizona built San Xavier del Bac for the glory of God. Despite a lack of material and technology, their work, finished in 1797, stands today as a place revered by both worshipers and tourists.

Location: South Tucson.
Description: The historic "White Dove of the Desert," with a congregation founded in 1692 and an active Catholic parish serving members of the Tohono O'odham Nation.
How to get there: From I-19, go west on San Xavier Road (Exit 92). Follow the signs to the mission, about 1 mile away and visible from a distance.

The church has been called one of the best examples of Spanish Colonial architecture in the United States, and the accomplishment is stunning. Despite the presence of many tourists, an atmosphere of reverence prevails in this space where prayers first were said more than 200 years ago. The smell of decades of incense lingers in the air. You might be moved to pray or snap pictures or simply gaze, inspired by angels and saints depicted on the walls in brilliant reds, blues, and gold. For an answer to a prayer, you can light a candle or pin a photograph to the satin blanket covering a life-size, reclining statue of St. Francis Xavier.

Because San Xavier's priest refused to pledge loyalty to the Mexican government in the 1820s, the church was abandoned and fell into ruins. A modern-day, multimillion-dollar preservation project salvaged it, and ongoing restoration efforts continue at the church, now listed on the National Register of Historic Places.

No plans are in place to complete the east bell tower, however, which the original builders left unfinished most likely because the project ran out of money. Legends surround the tower, including one of a worker who fell from it to his death. The story tells that he turned into a rattlesnake and made his home there, so the Native American builders chose to stay away.

Situated on lands of the Tohono O'odham Nation, the mission is an active parish, and Masses are held almost daily along with other celebrations. The church is open from 8 a.m. to 6 p.m. daily and donations are accepted.

If you arrive early, you will enjoy cooler summer temperatures and more solitude, uninterrupted save for the photographers who set up their equipment in the parking lot to capture the church in the perfect morning light. Don't skip the museum, which displays historic photographs and timelines that illustrate the history behind this holy place where every architectural detail holds meaning. Indian cuisine and craft shops surrounding the grounds also cater to church visitors.

37. San José de Tumacácori Mission Church

Tumacácori National Historical Park
1891 E. Frontage Rd.
Tumacácori, AZ 85640
(520) 398-2341
E-mail: TUMA_interpretation@nps.gov
www.nps.gov/tuma

*I*n the late 17th century, the Jesuits and then the Franciscans brought Christianity and the Roman Catholic Church to the ancestors of the present-day O'odham tribes. Established in 1691 by Father Eusebio Kino, San José de Tumacácori was the first mission in what is now Arizona.

A small chapel was built on the site in 1757. When the Franciscans started construction on the church at Tumacácori in 1800, they envisioned a sanctuary as grand and striking as its sister parish to the north, Mission San Xavier del Bac. By 1822, the church was in use, but just six years later, the Mexican government evicted the last Spanish priest there. In 1848, the Mexican priests and Native American parishioners abandoned the church and left it to the elements and vandalism.

Location: Tumacácori, about 18 miles north of Nogales and the Mexican border.
Description: The oldest mission site in Arizona; features a partially finished mission church.
How to get there: From Tucson, drive south on I-19 for 45 miles. Exit at Tumacácori (Exit 29) and follow the signs.

In the tradition of the great cathedrals, the church originally was designed in the shape of a cross. However, the structure was not finished and now looks like a long hall. The interior is remarkably well preserved, despite having been partially without a roof for 60 years. Weather has exposed the adobe bricks in some places, but the church still maintains an imposing presence on the flat grasslands. Although the colorful altar has faded, traces of the blue and red colors decorating the plaster walls still linger. The thick walls cool the interior, even in summer.

The museum gives a historical overview of the area and the church. Still, much is left to your imagination. You can take a guided tour during the winter months or a self-guided tour year-round. Often, local artists demonstrate crafts here and fresh tortillas are made in the courtyard while you watch.

Twice each year, the church comes alive with a Historic High Mass, the *Misa Mayor*. Visitors must dress in traditional Spanish or Native American clothing of the 17th and 18th centuries, so leave your wristwatch at home. Advance reservations are required. Traditionally, the High Mass was sung in Latin and the sermon was given in Spanish or the native language. People stood during services because the facility lacked pews or benches.

For the benefit of its preservation, the site was designated a national monument in 1908 and became a national historical park in 1990. Efforts to stabilize the structure began in 1919 and continue today through the park's preservation program. The park is open 8 a.m. to 5 p.m. daily except Christmas and Thanksgiving, and the grounds are wheelchair accessible.

Retreats

38. Redemptorist Retreat and Renewal Center at Picture Rocks

7101 W. Picture Rocks Rd.
Tucson, AZ 85743
(520) 744-3400
www.desertrenewal.org

Mailing address:
P.O. Box 569
Cortaro, AZ 85652

*N*ot far from the clean, comfortable Redemptorist Retreat and Renewal Center at Picture Rocks, petroglyphs pecked into boulders by the Hohokam people hundreds of years ago testify to the area's ancient roots. The center's 120 acres border Saguaro National Park, with miles of desert trails awaiting exploration. You might choose to follow the Stations of the Cross along a steep trail or simply sit quietly in the center's chapel and pray.

Location: Border of Tucson and Cortaro.

Description: A Catholic retreat center marked by solitude in the desert; welcomes visitors of all faiths.

How to get there: From I-10, take Cortaro Road (Exit 246) southwest and go almost 2 miles. Go right (west) on Ina Road for almost 0.5 mile. Go left (south) on Wade Road for almost 1 mile. Go right (west) on Picture Rocks Road for about 0.25 mile. The retreat center will be on your left, across from the Desert House of Prayer.

The Scripture on the chapel wall paraphrases Hosea 2:14: "The desert will lead you to your heart where I will speak." People of Biblical times knew that the voice of God rings clearly in the desert, as do the Redemptorists of the Denver Province, who run the Retreat and Renewal Center and the Desert House of Prayer across the street (see p. 105). Although the Redemptorists are a Catholic order, they welcome guests of all religious traditions to the center.

Private prayer and regular liturgical celebrations take place in the chapel. On weekdays, silent meditation is scheduled from 6:45 a.m. to 7:15 a.m., followed by praying the Psalms and concluding with the Eucharist. On Saturdays, the Eucharist and Perpetual Help Devotions commence at 7:30 a.m.; on Sundays, the Eucharist and Holy Days of Obligation are at 10:30 a.m.

The center hosts a variety of events, including writer's workshops; programs for women and seniors; and private, directed, and contemplative retreats. Private retreatants can schedule time for spiritual direction with a staff member. One of the directed retreats employs the methods of the 12-step recovery program. The contemplative option combines periods of meditation with work, prayer, silent meals, and lectures and private meetings with an instructor. The tradition of contemplation honors an ancient Christian practice that mirrors the life of Jesus: Through times of silence and of work, one can fulfill Jesus' teaching in the book of Matthew to "love your God with all your heart, all your soul, all your strength, and all your mind, and love your neighbor as yourself."

The retreat center is not a resort but a place for spiritual growth and nourishment. However, it does offer more amenities than many retreat facilities, such as a library and 50 private rooms with baths. Linens are provided and you are asked to make up the bed with clean linens before you leave. The individual rooms do not have phones, but a pay phone is

available in the room adjoining the dining hall, along with a modem connection, newspapers, and snacks. Leaders on group retreats are assigned a
voice mailbox and messages for retreatants are posted on a message board.
Emergency messages will be delivered to you immediately, no matter what
time of day.

The buffet-style meals consist of simple, healthy food. The main meal
is at noon and lighter fare is served for supper.

The costs per room vary, but start at about $50 for a midweek private
room and go up for weekends, double occupancy, and suites. Meeting
rooms for groups also are available.

Guests are asked to respect the quiet and solitude considered essential
here. You're also expected to refrain from climbing the rocks where the
petroglyphs are to avoid damaging their historical value and disturbing
their sacred nature. The instability of the rocks along the wash also makes
them unsafe to climb.

Call between 8:30 a.m. and 4:30 p.m. Mondays through Fridays to
make your arrangements.

39. Desert House of Prayer

7350 W. Picture Rocks Rd.   **Mailing address:**
Tucson, AZ 85743   P.O. Box 570
(520) 744-3825   Cortaro, AZ 85652
www.desertrenewal.org

Along the narrow road leading up to the Desert House of Prayer, a simple sign greets you: "No hunting except for peace." In the silence that surrounds this place of contemplative prayer, you're sure to find serenity and a way to connect with the divine.

Desert House of Prayer's chapel, lodge, and hermitages merge with nature. During your stay, mule deer might bound across your path or a mother javelina might take her babies for a walk. You might spy a rattlesnake slithering by or watch hawks circling high overhead. As you draw closer to God through quiet prayer and silence, your awareness of God's presence in nature will grow. The retreat center was built to impact

Location: Border of Tucson and Cortaro.

Description: A Catholic-run center for silent retreats in a natural desert; visitors of all faiths are welcome.

How to get there: From I-10, take Cortaro Road (Exit 246) southwest and go almost 2 miles. Go right (west) on Ina Road for almost 0.5 mile. Go left (south) on Wade Road for almost 1 mile. Go right (west) on Picture Rocks Road for about 0.25 mile. The retreat center will be on your right, across from Redemptorist Retreat and Renewal Center at Picture Rocks.

the desert as little as possible and, as one sister in residence says, they would never kill a rattlesnake.

Desert House of Prayer accommodates only individuals or married couples for its retreats, which might last two or three days or continue for months, depending on availability and the needs of the retreatant. When you come here, don't expect a resort—this is a tidy, cozy place in a community committed to silence. The retreat center is Catholic but welcomes all visitors.

The chapel's open windows frame the desert. The chapel bears the name Our Lady of Solitude, a reminder that Mary could not have become the mother of Jesus without silence because only those who are silent hear the word of God.

Next to a large, green, blank book, a hand-lettered sign invites you to write requests and the community will pray for you. Dozens of handwritten messages fill the book: prayers for safe trips, for family, for the health of those with cancer, and "for my grandchildren, that they will grow in the love of God." Tiny Stations of the Cross, set with turquoise, line the wall. At the Station where Jesus dies, a red-orange stone replaces the blue stone.

Communal prayers and Mass take place in the chapel, as well as centering prayer, a Christian adaptation of the Soto Zen method of meditation. Different from prayers of petition, praise, or intercession, centering prayer is praying without words. In stillness, you wait for God to speak to you. On Saturday nights, you can schedule private time in the chapel for adoration and prayer with the Blessed Sacrament. In addition to the chapel, guests are free to use the library, which houses more than 11,000 volumes.

In 1974, the Redemptorists of the Denver Province, a Catholic order, founded the Desert House of Prayer at the location across the street, now home to the Redemptorist Retreat and Renewal Center at Picture Rocks (see p. 102). To provide a facility with more silence, they built the current Desert House of Prayer at its present site in 1979. The fact that the walk to retrieve the morning newspaper is 0.3 mile testifies to the remoteness of this place.

During the week, breakfast and lunch take place in silence; talking is allowed at supper, except for Fridays. Each Friday, "Hermit Day" is observed with fasting and complete silence. Hermit Day pays homage to Christ's passion and death, and also makes a show of support for victims of injustice and those who work for peace.

The guest rooms are silent areas, except during designated conversation times. Desert House of Prayer offers 10 motel-style rooms with private baths, as well as five hermitages. All rooms have single beds except for one with a double bed, purchased for the center by a married couple on retreat. Glass patio doors open to uninterrupted stretches of desert and the dark night sky reveals every constellation. Of course, no rooms have phones or televisions.

Rooms are about $50 per night, per person, including three meals. With double beds, a kitchenette, and private, full baths, hermitages cost a little more. Some of the hermitages have fireplaces. Accommodations here typically book six months in advance, so call ahead.

In such a fast-paced world, it's often hard to find silence, but people from across the globe discover space to think and to pray at Desert House of Prayer.

40. Holy Trinity Monastery

P.O. Box 298
Saint David, AZ 85630
(520) 720-4642
www.holytrinitymonastery.org

*L*ong before you arrive at Holy Trinity Monastery, you see the 70-foot Celtic cross that towers over the 132-acre community along the San Pedro River. At the base of the cross is a relic of the True Cross, given to the monastery for safekeeping. Passersby often see the cross and, if the monastery can accommodate last-minute drop-ins, join in the community's life of work and prayer for an afternoon or an extended retreat.

The river here nurtures cottonwoods and pecan trees, making this a lush oasis in the high desert. The property boasts a 1.3-mile hiking trail through a designated bird sanctuary. Sprinkled throughout are venues for quiet reflection such as the Stations of the Cross, a Japanese-themed garden, shady ponds, and the shrine to Our Lady of Medjugorje.

Our Lady of Guadalupe Church was dedicated in 1981. The mission-style, rammed-earth church has a green copper bell hanging under its cross. Inside, the altar is of twisted wood. Light filters in through leaded glass windows.

The Olivetan Benedictine community, which founded the monastery in 1974, follows the rule of "work and pray." They farm, harvest pecans, and keep sheep, chickens, and cows. As a guest, you are expected to keep the monastery's schedule of prayer and spiritual reading, and to observe the hours of silence.

Location: Saint David, 58 miles southeast of Tucson.
Description: A silent, secluded place for Catholic or non-Catholic retreats in a monastic community.
How to get there: From I-10, take Exit 303 at Benson. Go south 9 miles on AZ 80 and look for the cross and the sign past Saint David. The monastery is between mileposts 302 and 303.

The monastery hosts conferences, tours, and group and private retreats, both Catholic and non-Catholic. If you are Roman Catholic, you may receive the Eucharist during Mass. People with other backgrounds may receive a blessing during Communion; non-Catholics identify themselves by crossing their arms across their chest when they come forward. Spiritual direction and the Sacrament of Reconciliation are available upon request. A Taizé candlelight service takes place on Fridays.

Holy Trinity provides basic linens and three meals a day. The 11 rooms fill quickly, so you are encouraged to make your plans well ahead of time; weekend group retreats are often booked a year in advance. In the hermitage, you'll find a single bed, private bath, microwave, small refrigerator, and a cross hanging on the wall. The hermitage's porch overlooks the pond, where black swans swim. No phones, radios, or televisions are allowed. In case of an emergency, your family may contact you through the guest coordinator. The monastery's RV park accommodates visitors with campers. All retreatants can check out books from the 50,000-volume library.

Suggested prices for retreats start at $35 per person and $60 per couple, per day. Stays in the hermitage are $50 daily and $900 monthly. Holy Trinity does not want the cost to discourage someone from making a retreat, so the proprietors advise anyone who cannot afford the donation to contact the guest coordinator. The grounds are also open for day visits and the gift shop offers goods made at the monastery.

41. Santa Rita Abbey

HC 1 Box 929
Sonoita, AZ 85637
(520) 455-5595
www.santaritabbey.org

*T*he nuns of the Cistercian Order of the Strict Observance devote themselves to contemplation and worship of God. In silence, solitude, prayer, and simplicity, they follow the example of St. Benedict. Such a path is offered to those who come to Santa Rita Abbey's retreat house in search of privacy and peace. The pervasive quiet heals the spirit, connects the self with a transcendent world, and allows the mind to focus and think.

Thomas Merton, a modern-day Cistercian monk, writes of the way of life: "There is in all things an inexhaustible sweetness and purity, a silence

Location: Near Sonoita, about an hour southeast of Tucson.
Description: A retreat house and church in a community of Cistercian nuns living a life of prayer and work.
How to get there: Take I-10 east to AZ 83 (Exit 281). Go south 21 miles on AZ 83 toward Sonoita. Just past milepost 38, about 4 miles before Sonoita, go right (west) on Gardner Canyon Road (County Road 92). After 1 mile, go right (north) on Fish Canyon Road (CR 163). Go 1 mile, take the left at the fork in the road, and check in at the monastery.

that is a fountain of action and of joy. It rises up in wordless gentleness and flows out to me from the unseen roots of all created beings."

In the inviting retreat house, each comfortable room has a private bath. The simple chapel in the retreat house brings the outdoors inside with its large windows and unending view of the desert.

The abbey hosts both individual and group retreats, and the suggested donation is $25 per day. Guests are asked to arrive before 7 p.m. Food is provided, but retreatants make their own meals in a common kitchen.

In this community founded in 1972, the sisters earn a living by making altar breads, candles, and other crafts. They sell 100-percent whole wheat altar breads to more than 300 parishes throughout the United States.

Both locals and travelers join the sisters for Mass on the weekends. The sisters also welcome serious inquiries from anyone interested in becoming a nun. According to the website, candidates should be "sincerely desirous of seeking God in a life of simplicity and prayer."

For retreat reservations, please call between 9 a.m. and 4 p.m., or send a letter to the attention of the guest mistress.

42. Tree of Life Rejuvenation Center

P.O. Box 1080
Patagonia, AZ 85624
(520) 394-2520
www.treeoflife.nu

*E*verything at Tree of Life Rejuvenation Center leads to spiritual awakening. The site is home to some vortexes, and the sacred practices by the people living and visiting here have imbued the land with spiritual energy.

Tree of Life sprawls across 166 acres on a mesa at about 4,000 feet, with views of higher mountains and the yellow grass of southern Arizona, which turns green in July or August if there's enough rain. The center accommodates 16 people in eight rooms, and offers an eclectic mix of programs and retreats.

A holistic medical doctor and spiritual facilitator, Tree of Life director Gabriel Cousens has been called a "yogi of real spiritual attainment" by Swami Prakashananda. Dr. Cousens has authored several books including *Spiritual Nutrition and the Rainbow Diet*. He founded the center on the idea that for people to make real changes in their lives, they need a direct, positive awakening of the body, the emotions, and the spirit. To do that, they need to spend time connecting with the ancient energies of the earth and looking for divinity within.

Location: Patagonia, about an hour and a half southeast of Tucson.

Description: A healing eco-retreat center to create vitality, harmony, and renewal of the body, mind, and spirit.

How to get there: Take I-10 east to AZ 83, Exit 281. Go south on AZ 83 to Sonoita. From there, go right (southwest) on AZ 82 to Patagonia. You need to call ahead to make final arrangements to get to the center, which is located near the town.

In 1992, Gabriel founded a nonprofit church/temple dedicated to humanitarian service, the Essene Order of Light. By drawing from different spiritual traditions including Native American, Shamanic Judaism, and Essene Christian mysticism, Tree of Life helps people find their inner selves. This exercise can take more than one path, as reflected in the diversity of traditions espoused here.

The temple features a pyramid roof and large crystal set inside a Star of David. On Friday nights, a Kabbalistic Shabbat service in the mystical Jewish tradition takes place, with prayers in Hebrew. You also might participate in a sweat lodge during every new moon, Sanskrit chanting, or a goddess circle. A labyrinth and an outdoor mikvah, the ritual cleansing pool in Judaism, are being added.

In the afternoon, six days a week, you can do yoga on the outdoor platform with stunning views in all directions. In the evening, you can sit with the others, watch the sun set, and send peace out to the planet.

Even the food serves as part of the spiritual renewal—some retreats center on fasting to detoxify and cleanse the body so the energy can come through. Following the theory that cooking destroys food's enzymes and energy, all the cuisine served here is live (uncooked), vegan, and 100-percent organic.

A variety of retreats and workshops are offered along with additional health consultations with Dr. Cousens. Prices start around $400 for a two-night stay to a weeklong purification retreat for $2,500. A seven-day personal fasting retreat is $1,036. The center also presents classes on live-food preparation, spiritual gardening, and Reiki, among other topics.

43. Diamond Mountain

P.O. Box 37
Bowie, AZ 85605
(520) 847-1213
www.diamondmtn.org

*I*n October 2001, Diamond Mountain purchased a 1,000-acre property known as Bear Springs Ranch, nestled in the northern foothills of the Chiricahua Mountains and adjoining Fort Bowie National Historic Site. Construction of a small temple and several residences began in 2002.

The mission of Diamond Mountain is to provide all the internal and external conditions necessary for a person to reach total enlightenment for the sake of others in this lifetime. Specifically, Diamond Mountain serves as a place for serious dharma practitioners to live ethical, simple, and undistracted lives within a spiritual community. As part of this lifestyle, community members dedicate substantial time and energy each day to meditation, study, and service to others.

Location: About 10 miles south of Bowie, which is about 2 hours east of Tucson.
Description: A 1,000-acre retreat property for serious dharma practitioners.
How to get there: Take I-10 east to Bowie. Go right (south) on Apache Pass Road for 10 miles. Go left (south) on the Handicapped Access Road to Fort Bowie. Because of the limited resources available at this time, visitors must call ahead.

Diamond Mountain is one of many projects of Geshe Michael Roach, the first American to earn a geshe (doctor of theology) degree from the traditional schools of Tibetan Buddhism currently located in India. Geshe Michael's goal is to translate and transmit the pure lineage of authentic teachings into the English language and American cultural environment while preserving their native origins.

Diamond Mountain brings highly qualified masters of Tibetan Buddhism here to teach and pass on priceless spiritual knowledge. Courses from the Asian Classics Institute—founded by Geshe Michael with spiritual guidance from Tibetan Buddhist master Khen Rinpoche Geshe Lobsang Tharchin— are taught frequently at Diamond Mountain, along with a variety of prayer, meditation, and extended study courses. The programs are open to all spiritually motivated people.

Diamond Mountain is open to the public for free teachings on Buddhist philosophy and logic, but participants must make reservations in advance. It also hosts four-day Quiet Retreat Teachings, free with a $10–$100 registration fee, depending on what the retreatant can comfortably afford. Visitors to Diamond Mountain arrange for their own food and lodging.

Sacred Places

44. Casa Grande Ruins National Monument

1100 Ruins Dr.
Coolidge, AZ 85228
(520) 723-3172
E-mail: CAGR_Superintendent@nps.gov
www.nps.gov/cagr

Casa Grande Ruins
Out of the Earth I rose.
Built to watch the land.
Constructed by hand,
Destroyed by time,
And here I still stand.
Faintly remembering what once used to be.
—*Leland Thomas, 2001*

$\mathcal{M}$aybe the Hohokam people held ceremonial dances and rites in front of the Great House. Perhaps the brownish-yellow structure, emerging from the same-colored earth, marked the seasons, with its summer solstice hole and its fall and spring lunar equinox alignments. The massive, four-story building could have been a place of learning, a lookout, or a communal gathering spot for the surrounding village—or all of these.

For Leland Thomas, an O'odham and Casa Grande park ranger, the mysterious dwelling gives him a sacred connection to his people's ancient past. Through his tours, he shares traditional stories and original poetry inspired by Casa Grande to help visitors understand the place beyond its historical significance.

He writes of Casa Grande and its builders, "Touch my walls, you'll feel the strength that built me. Stand silent, you'll hear them in my rooms. Close your eyes, you'll surely see them. The ancient Hohokam."

Casa Grande—the largest Hohokam structure still standing today—was set aside by the U.S. government as an archaeological preserve in 1892. It was the first site to receive this designation. The first European known to have seen Casa Grande was Captain Juan Mateo Manje, who noted the discovery in his journal in 1697.

The structure represents an amazing accomplishment without modern technology. The house is made of caliche, which is like a natural concrete, with 11 rooms and walls 4.5 feet thick at the base. Handprints of the builders still linger on some of the walls, which also bear graffiti dating back to the late 1800s and early 1900s. Evidence of nearby villages and a ball court surround the Great House.

A ramada-like shelter protects Casa Grande from the elements. Through the years, no alterations have been made except to stabilize the foundation; 85 percent of the structure is original.

Location: Coolidge, about an hour northwest of Tucson and halfway to Phoenix.

Description: The United States' first archaeological preserve, which protects a four-story prehistoric ruin built of caliche mud by the Hohokam in the 1300s.

How to get there: From I-10, take Exit 194 and follow AZ 287 east to AZ 87. Turn left (north) on AZ 87 and follow it through Coolidge and on to the monument. Alternatively, from I-10, take Exit 185 and go east on AZ 387 to AZ 87, where you'll turn right and continue to the monument. Signs on AZ 87 mark the way to Casa Grande. The Visitors' Center and ruins are at the end of Ruins Drive, an almost mile-long paved road west of AZ 87.

Archaeologists speculate about the fate of the Hohokam, who apparently disappeared in the 15th century, leaving behind few clues except for an elaborate canal system that likely watered their crops. Thomas, who lives in the Gila River Indian Community, doesn't wonder. He believes they were ancestors of the present-day Akimel and Tohono O'odham. "Some of us don't believe the Hohokam went anywhere," he explains. "We're still here. We have the same type of pottery design and methods. We eat the same types of foods."

Park rangers such as Thomas lead regular tours of the ruins from January through April, or you can take a self-guided tour. Guided tours the rest of the year depend on staff availability, so call ahead. Special tours and events take place during Arizona State Archaeology Month in March and Native American Month in November.

Admission to Casa Grande Ruins National Monument is $3 per person, and visitors 16 and younger are free. Hours are 8 a.m. to 5 p.m. every day except Christmas. The short trails are wheelchair accessible. Be prepared for heat in the summer, as temperatures soar above 100 degrees.

45. Garden of Gethsemane

602 W. Congress St.
Tucson, AZ 85745
(520) 791-5890

As he lay critically injured on a World War I battlefield, Felix Lucero made a promise to God. According to a plaque in Tucson's Garden of Gethsemane, he "vowed to God and himself that he would dedicate the remainder of his life to making religious statues."

Lucero's life-size, white concrete statues of Jesus on the cross, the Last Supper, Mary and Joseph, and others occupy the shady, brick-paved garden courtyard known as the Garden of Gethsemane. The Knights of Columbus maintain the statue collection, a Tucson landmark since 1945. The statues were moved to their present location near the Santa Cruz River Walk in 1971.

Benches invite you to sit and pray for a while. A plaque explains Lucero's ambition behind creating the statues. People leave flowers, rosaries, and notes behind.

The City of Tucson has targeted the area for revitalization, but homeless people sometimes congregate near the park, which is surrounded by a fence that is locked at night. The Garden of Gethsemane is open seven days a week from 8 a.m. to 3:30 p.m. and can be reserved for special occasions. The multilevel courtyard is wheelchair accessible.

Location: Central Tucson.
Description: A garden park with large religious statues.
How to get there: From I-10, go west on Congress Street (Exit 258) just past the Santa Cruz River. The park is at the corner of Bonita Avenue and Congress Street.

46. El Tiradito Shrine

400 S. Main Ave.
Tucson, AZ 85701

*F*or more than a century, candles have burned at Tucson's "Wishing Shrine," El Tiradito. The dirt surrounding the three-walled shrine appears wet, from so much melted wax, and smoke darkens the walls.

It's likely the only shrine dedicated to a sinner, not a saint—at least in the entire Southwest. El Tiradito translates as "outcast" or "fallen one." Stories vary about the shrine, but most agree that it was built in the 1870s after Juan Oliveras, a young sheepherder, was caught in a love triangle and killed with an ax by the jealous husband.

Oliveras was buried near the current location of the shrine because he couldn't be interred in the consecrated ground of the Catholic cemetery, the story goes. As people lit candles in the vicinity and prayed for his soul, the shrine got its start.

Location: Central Tucson.

Description: A historic shrine in Barrio Viejo.

How to get there: From I-10, go east on Congress Street (Exit 258) for about 0.75 mile. Go right (south) on Church Avenue and continue about 0.5 mile. Turn right (west) on Simpson Street and go about 0.5 mile. Turn right (north) on Main Avenue. The shrine is in a vacant lot next to the El Minuto Café, 354 S. Main Ave., between Simpson Street and Cushing Street.

According to the legend, if you light a candle there that burns through the night and into the next morning, your wish will be granted. Along with the candles, people leave flowers, notes, pictures, and other mementos at the shrine. The shrine, which is listed on the National Register of Historic Places, has become a revered place to pray, and locals attribute many answered prayers to its power.

47. Baboquivari Mountains

Tohono O'odham Nation
Baboquivari District Office
Near Sells, AZ
(520) 383-2366

*A*t 7,730 feet, Baboquivari Peak soars above southern Arizona's Baboquivari Mountains. Within this range are I'ito's Cave and the origin of the Tohono O'odham people. The creation story tells that I'ito, which means "creator," brought the people out from the underworld through a cave hidden away in the piñon and oaks of the mountains.

Location: Near Sells, about 65 miles southwest of Tucson.

Description: A park near sacred mountains.

How to get there: From I-19, go west about 60 miles on AZ 86 (Exit 99) to Sells. Take the first exit into Sells and go left (south) through town. The road curves, taking you to Indian Route 19. Turn left and go south for about 12 miles, past Topawa, until you see a park building and a sign for Indian Route 10. Go left (east) on Indian Route 10, a dirt road, and continue about 10 miles to the park. The dirt road is suitable for high-clearance and four-wheel-drive vehicles.

Anyone can use the campgrounds and picnic areas, and hike the trails, but I'ito's Cave is strictly off-limits to non-tribal members. Many Native American sacred sites are closed to outsiders to protect holy places from vandalism and other threats.

In years past, some Tucson natives told stories of taking gifts to I'ito's Cave with the belief that for those who were pure of heart, I'ito would grant their requests. The cave was filled with pictures, a basketball, and all sorts of tokens left behind.

But today, that would be trespassing. Non-tribal members who have recently paid a visit to the Baboquivari Mountains have noted that the spiritual energy simply emanating from this sacred range provides enough reason to go there, while still respecting the integrity of the holy site.

Region Three

Prescott and
West-Central Arizona

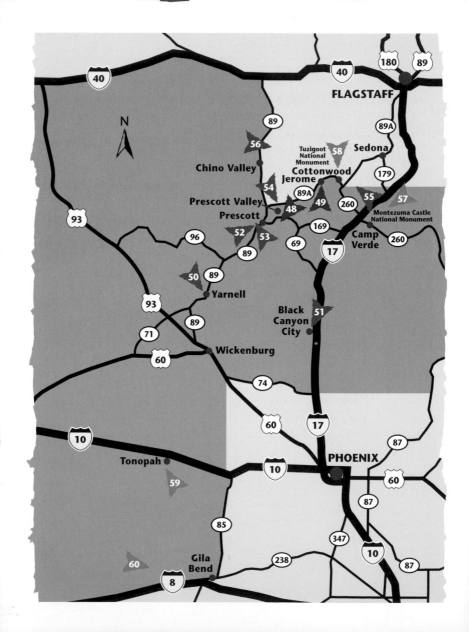

$\mathcal{P}$rescott and west-central Arizona might have fewer residents than other areas of the state, but the region's immense charm and cooler climate draw many city refugees each year. Summertime temperatures hover much lower than in Phoenix and Tucson, and winters bring snow—sometimes a dusting, sometimes a few inches.

The Prescott area, in particular, is a mecca for church camps and retreat centers. More than 30 exist in the area, about half of which have a religious affiliation. Most of the camps host specific churches or denominations and are open only to their own members; such camps are not included in this book. Camps that take outside groups are featured in these pages. Rustic accommodations define some retreat centers, while others cater to adults who really would rather not sleep on the top bunk or share a bathroom. A few have

expanded their facilities in recent years to serve the growing number of adults who find value in getting away to the woods, yet prefer that their journeys through the pines keep to paved roads.

The more popular places book a year in advance, so always call ahead. However, camps can often make room for individuals and smaller groups, and last-minute cancellations might create availability.

Destinations of note pepper the area west of Arizona's central corridor. The Shrine of St. Joseph of the Mountains long has been a popular stop for prayer and reflection, and retreat facilities now welcome those who wish to stay longer. Painted Rocks Petroglyph Site west of Gila Bend provides a solitary experience along with an up-close look at ancient rock carvings. And El Dorado Hot Spring in Tonopah, with its clothing-optional areas, gives the unabashed the opportunity to *really* get back to nature.

Though not a physical destination, Christ Unlimited Ministries—run from an old church camp in Cherry by former nondenominational church leaders Bud and Betty Miller—maintains one of the world's largest Christian websites, www.bible.com. From the site, Web surfers can read and search the Bible in a dozen English translations and more than 50 other languages. In one recent month, the site received 23 million visits. During the dot-com craze, the Millers were offered $1 million for the domain name, but they declined. "It would be hard to explain to God why we sold it for retirement," says Bud. "We know God wants us to use this to touch lives." For these Arizona-based cyber-missionaries, it's the spiritual destination that matters most.

Chapel of the Valley, Prescott Valley

Sanctuaries

48. Chapel of the Valley

2215 N. Fifth St.
Prescott Valley, AZ 86314
(928) 775-0552

*C*hapel of the Valley is the realization of the dream of Arizona pioneer and rancher Johnie Lee Fain. Perched on a hill in the park named for her family, the charming brick chapel showcases stained-glass windows built in Germany in 1906.

That same year, Johnie Lee was born in Texas. She moved with her family to the Prescott area when she was 12. She studied piano at the Fort Worth Conservatory, worked for a bank, and was going to work for a U.S. oil company in Mexico until Norman Fain, her high-school sweetheart, proposed at Stanford University. She accepted and they married in 1928. As the wife of a rancher, she raised three children while she worked the ranch the same as any cowboy. She volunteered for the Red Cross during World War II, raised money for community causes, and played piano for her church.

In 1913, the stained-glass windows currently at Chapel of the Valley were installed in the chapel at Prescott Mercy Hospital, now Prescott College. When the chapel burned decades ago, the windows were put up for sale. A local man named Henry Brooks bought one window and took out a loan to purchase the rest of the eight windows. For years, he stored the windows in his home.

He and Johnie Lee Fain became great friends, and she shared with him her vision of creating a chapel, a place of beauty and happiness. Should such a chapel be built, they decided, the windows would serve as its centerpiece. Fain died in 1999, but one of her daughters, Carolyn Sue Fain, and her family saw Johnie's dream

Location: Prescott Valley.
Description: A charming non-denominational chapel with historic stained-glass windows.
How to get there: From AZ 69, go south on Prescott East Highway. After a block, go left (east) on Second Street. Go right (south) on Fifth Street, which ends at Fain Park. The chapel is on a hill near the entrance to the park.

through to fruition. Carolyn Sue, who donated the money to build the chapel, died the year before the chapel's dedication on April 7, 2002.

The nondenominational chapel sits in Fain Park, a 100-acre property with hiking trails, fishing, a pond and bridge, and covered ramadas for picnics. The shade trees loom tall above the cool green grass. On the chapel's dedication monument, Johnie Lee Fain's words are written so all might understand her desire to create "a place of beauty filled with the spirit of God and his capacity to meet the needs of all who visit.... May hope and inspiration unfold within you as you search for truth. Make the most of life's journey, for it is your gift to give. Go forward and trust in God."

Inside the chapel, the jewel-toned windows depict Jesus and the saints, and the colors glow pure when the light shines through. Everything in the chapel exudes understated elegance. Nothing detracts from the beauty of the windows. The chapel's maple floor bears a diagonal pattern in white oak, and beams span the open ceiling. The chapel seats 48 in wooden chairs. Cases in the chapel's foyer display photos of Johnie at various stages in her life.

Currently, the chapel is open 10 a.m. to 5 p.m. on Saturday and Sunday, and by special appointment. The goal is to expand the chapel's operating hours and to open it for weddings and other occasions. Only handicapped parking is available near the chapel, but the park has plenty of parking and the chapel is just a short walk up the hill.

49. Holy Family Catholic Church

101 N. County Rd.
Jerome, AZ 86331
(928) 649-0929

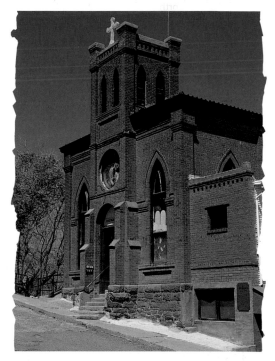

In Arizona, few towns are quite as eccentric as Jerome, so it's only appropriate that a colorful tale surrounds its Catholic church. Built precariously on the side of Cleopatra Hill, Jerome was one of many boomtowns fueled by the mining industry. By 1900, the town had nearly 3,000 residents, making it among the largest in the Arizona Territory.

Many male workers lost their lives in the mines, while prostitution was a leading career choice among women. Of course, a church was needed to counter the influences of liquor and loose women. If the churchgoers couldn't save the souls of their neighbors, they could at least pray for them.

The current Holy Family Catholic Church was completed around 1898 after the first church fell victim to one of several fires that swept through the town. The church bustled with activity and the brick building was the pride of the largely Hispanic parish community.

By the 1950s, the church no longer served as an active parish, and the mines and smelters had closed. The church fell into disrepair, although a resident priest remained, a Franciscan considered a bit odd by the handful of town residents left. The full extent of the Rev. Juan Atucha's eccentricities did not come to light until after his death in 1979.

Location: Jerome.

Description: A Catholic church with a colorful history.

How to get there: Take AZ 89A through Jerome. The church will be where North County Road and Hill Street veer off from AZ 89A. Parking is by the gift shop.

Atucha had worked as Holy Family's pastor for more than 30 years. When he died, parishioners found $60,000 in small change and bills hidden throughout the church and rectory in cans and bags. They never knew if the money came from church collections or Atucha's side income of repairing cars, but the parishioners put the money to good use. They restored the church, then reopened it in 1980 as a retreat center for Catholic groups. Today, the church is open daily to tourists, who walk across the creaky wood floors and take time to leave prayer requests in a basket by the altar.

The original glass windows slightly distort the outside view. Some of them bear etchings such as the keys to heaven and a dove, a symbol of the Holy Spirit. The altar and other parts of the church have also endured since it first opened. White-painted pressed tin covers the walls and ceilings. Bright blue accents the white, and gold adds richness to the altar.

For the non-Catholic, a prayer that explains the tradition of lighting candles is posted in English and Spanish. Not only was it appropriate for its original parishioners, it still speaks to those who stop by while visiting the artists' galleries and tourist attractions in Jerome:

> Oh Lord God, let this candle that I burn here be the light that leads me in my difficulties and decisions. Let it be the fire that burns all selfishness, pride and impurity in us. Let it be the flame that warms my heart. I cannot stay long in this your house; by letting this candle burn, it is part of myself I want to give you. Help me to carry on my prayer in today's and all my life's activities. Amen.

Holy Presents Gift Shop, on the church's lower level, is open most days. For information about the church's sacramental records, contact Immaculate Conception Parish, P.O. Box 995, Cottonwood, AZ 86326, or call (928) 634-2933.

Retreats

50. Shrine of St. Joseph of the Mountains Retreat and Conference Center

P.O. Box 267
Yarnell, AZ 85362
(928) 778-5229
www.stjoseph-shrine.org

*A*long a steep path carved into granite boulders, white concrete statues help to transport visitors back in time 2,000 years to Jesus' last days. In Arizona, the Shrine of St. Joseph of the Mountains is as close as you will get to the Via Dolorosa—the path that Christ walked in Jerusalem to his crucifixion. The route in the Holy Land buzzes with the activity of shops, loud noises, and pushy crowds. However, this setting half a world away provides a quiet and intimate experience, say those who have visited both places.

In the shade of oak trees, the walk begins with Jesus praying in the garden and the disciples gathered at the Last Supper, not traditionally part of the Stations of the Cross. Tall crosses mark the first 11 stations. Then, as you make your way up the mountain, you see the nearly life-size crucifix, with Jesus' blood-soaked head hanging in anguish. Vigil candles are not allowed at the stations, but people leave other tokens at this station such as flowers and pictures, tucked at Jesus' feet. The next station is a

Location: Yarnell, between Prescott and Wickenburg.
Description: An unusual Stations of the Cross, with life-size statues set in a landscape similar to Jerusalem; offers simple retreat facilities.
How to get there: Take AZ 89 to Yarnell. In town, turn west at the sign that says "Shrine of St. Joseph, 1/2 mile." The shrine is on the left side of the road and the House of Joseph Retreat Center is on the right. You will see the shrine before the retreat center houses, which are down a driveway and behind trees.

grief-stricken Mary embracing her lifeless son, followed by a cave tomb, where Jesus lies with eyes closed. A bronze statue of a resurrected Jesus anchors the courtyard at the beginning and end of your visit, reminding you of how Good Friday got its name. In the courtyard, you are free to light candles, sit on the benches, and pray.

The simple, white-painted sculptures differ from the ornate religious statuary found in some churches, but close inspection reveals that their details were painstakingly fashioned. Mary's veil falls around Jesus and tears flow down her face. Jesus' ribs protrude as he reclines in the cave tomb.

People tend to discover the shrine by accident or by word of mouth. The back road to Prescott is a curvy route popular among motorcycle enthusiasts and drivers of spiffy sports cars. Motorists notice the sign and turn onto the road to the shrine, then later bring back family and friends. Holy Week is the busiest time of year at Shrine of St. Joseph of the Mountains, but each month, hundreds of visitors from around the world find their way there.

The shrine's founders also discovered the site by chance while driving on what used to be US 89, which served as the main route to Prescott and California before the interstate highway system came into being. They stopped in Yarnell and stumbled upon the perfect place to create a shrine in appreciation of a favor granted by God. They sought no credit, only to honor Joseph—Jesus' foster father and the patron saint of happy families—and to create a setting to strengthen faith.

The statue of Joseph holding the Christ child was installed here first and the Stations were added in 1947. The only credit for the shrine is noted in a brochure: In 1939, the Catholic Action League of Arizona built the shrine. The Phoenix-based group, now disbanded, was organized to perform acts of mercy.

Acts of mercy also led to the establishment of a retreat center and lovely chapel on the property, as well as the shrine's continual upkeep. Volunteers renovated the buildings of a former school across the street from the shrine. The three houses and dining hall are a comfortable and reasonable place for group retreats both large and small. The current cost is about $15 per day, per person.

The gift shop is open from 11 a.m. to 5 p.m. most days and the shrine is open during daylight hours. A picnic area and public restrooms also are nearby. Shrine volunteers conduct no religious services at the site, but you may arrange to conduct your own services there by calling ahead.

51. Our Lady of Solitude Contemplative House of Prayer

P.O. Box 1140
Black Canyon City, AZ 85324
(623) 374-9204

*O*ffering views of mesas and miles of open desert, tiny cabins with deep porches perch on the side of the mountain. In the quiet, if you listen, God will speak to your heart. That's the purpose of Our Lady of Solitude Contemplative House of Prayer, a retreat center that takes only three individuals at a time—one per hermitage—for an experience of intense seclusion, quiet, and prayer.

In this contemplative setting, you will leave the world behind to focus only on prayer, Scripture reading, and God. Your sole occupation is to find solitude with God, which can be an overwhelming shift in a fast-paced world or a welcome opportunity for growth and discovery.

Retreatants gather together for a daily communion service or Mass in the meditation chapel. You spend the rest of your time alone, reading, praying, walking in the desert, sorting through the questions in your soul, and giving praise to God. Individual spiritual direction is available upon request. Retreatants receive a key to The Dwelling Place, a meditation chapel that offers an exposition of the Blessed Sacrament.

In 1984, Sister M. Therese Sedlock founded Our Lady of Solitude, part of the Roman Catholic Diocese of Phoenix. Our Lady of Solitude offers no day programs or classes, and Sister Therese asks that potential retreatants make all reservations in advance. Send your request by mail or call between 9 a.m. and noon on weekdays, but don't give up if you keep getting a busy signal. Sister Therese, who screens potential visitors over the phone, is quick to point out that such an experience is not for everyone. She desires to know why you want to come. "They have to want this kind of setting of silence and solitude," she explains.

Location: Near Black Canyon City, about 40 miles north of Phoenix.

Description: A small hermitage retreat center for a contemplative experience of intense solitude, silence, and prayer.

How to get there: From I-17, take Exit 242. Our Lady of Solitude is 1 mile from the exit. Take the frontage road on the east side and go right on St. Joseph Road (the first dirt road), which is marked by a tall transformer. Continue past the KOA campground. Use your vehicle's lowest gear on the steep ascent up St. Joseph Road. Close the gate at the bottom of the road before you go up the hill. You can also take a shuttle from Phoenix Sky Harbor International Airport and be picked up at Ron's Market in Black Canyon City.

The quiet environment attracts men and women of all ages from Catholic and other Christian backgrounds—but you will not get to know the others there. Total silence marks the hours. This experience, Sister Therese says, is a special time to be who you are and discover your gifts.

You can see the large cross by the bright white, round chapel from the interstate, but the steep, paved road to the hermitages and the main house are private. The main house has a library with more than 1,400 books and a large reading room with a fireplace. Each 13-by-13-foot hermitage is equipped with a bed, desk, chair, prayer corner, full bath, and two-sided prayer porch. The hermitages have electricity but no phones.

In the spring and fall, days are warm and nights are cool. Summer temperatures can reach more than 100 degrees. Each hermitage has a space heater and electric blanket, along with a fan and small wall-unit air conditioner.

Guests bring their own food and can use the small microwave, crock pot, toaster, and small refrigerator in each hermitage. Sister Therese recommends packing simple foods in keeping with the nature of the retreat: bread, peanut butter, jelly, canned goods, powdered milk, cereal, fruit, and juices.

Along with food, the recommended supply list includes a Bible and notebook, robe and slippers, personal items, bath soap, tissues, laundry detergent, flashlight, alarm clock, sunglasses, sturdy walking shoes, hat, and bed sheets and towels. Smoking and alcohol are prohibited.

The suggested donation per day is $25. A one-month stay is $600, and a three-month stay is $500 per month. Longer stays require a recommendation from your spiritual director.

52. Chapel Rock

1131 Country Club Dr.
Prescott, AZ 86303
(928) 445-3499
(602) 256-6021
E-mail: chapelrock@northlink.com
www.episcopal-az.org

*C*hapel Rock started in 1931 as a place for adults to escape Phoenix's brutally hot temperatures before air conditioning made summers in the city bearable. At Chapel Rock, the Episcopal bishop of Arizona kept a second home, now called Harte Lodge. The rest of the church quickly caught on. Diocese members bought the nearby complex of buildings formerly inhabited by a colony of tuberculosis patients, and the church camp was born.

The older buildings feel like the camp you might have attended as a kid, with sleeping rooms full of bunk beds and wooden-floored gathering rooms with rock fireplaces. The chapel, a place of prayer and worship featuring a rock cross and altar built into a granite outcropping, has served as the camp's focal point for decades.

Since 1997, though, the camp has been catering to adults once again. New lodges with private bathrooms have popped up on the 20-acre property and there's not a bunk bed in sight. The new retreat facilities equal those of a hotel and some rooms are wheelchair accessible. The adult lodges have self-contained meeting spaces.

The conference center is open year-round. Rooms are insulated and heated for a comfortable indoor climate even during the coldest winter days. At Chapel Rock, you feel secluded among the acres of ponderosa pines, oaks, and elms, yet you can still easily access town conveniences.

The camp and retreat center sleep 150 and meeting rooms accommodate more than 225 people in small and large rooms. An array of audio/visual equipment can be provided for meetings.

In St. Barnabas Lodge and St. James Lodge, each room has a single and a double bed, as well as a private bathroom and entrance. Another door leads to a private patio with forest views. These rooms cost about $44 per person, double occupancy, including three meals. Harte Lodge, the bishop's former home, has shared bathrooms and 15 single beds. The cost, $42 per person, also includes three meals. The staff serves cafeteria-style meals in the dining hall. For adult lodging, linens are provided, but you are asked to strip the bed before you go.

The camp offers horseback riding along with the use of ropes courses, sports equipment, and a ball field. Hiking trails await nearby.

Church staff members run the summer camp programs for youth. Kids populate the camp every week in the summertime, making it slightly noisier than other times. Still, adults have plenty of space to get away and relax while listening to the birds in the forest.

Church and other religious groups hold retreats here, as do secular groups. The popular Thanksgiving camp for families draws people of all ages. When extra space is available, individuals can book rooms for private, personal retreats.

53. Camp Pinerock

1400 Pine Dr.
Prescott, AZ 86303
(928) 445-8357
(623) 465-5938
E-mail: camppinerock@cableone.net
www.camppinerock.org

*A*s Arizona's urban centers have grown, people have felt an increasing need to swap their hectic schedules for the opportunity to breathe clean air, smell the pine trees, listen to the birds, and relax—and Camp Pinerock is an ideal spot for such an escape. For many, tuning into God comes more easily when they are alone and away from everyday distractions and commitments.

Inspired by the pines and the beauty of God's creation in nature, Camp Pinerock is a Christian camp through and through. Three crosses greet visitors and Bible verses decorate the auditorium walls. Although privately owned, the camp allows other Christian groups to hold retreats and camp programs on the premises. Catholic, evangelical Christian, and mainstream Protestant groups have used the facilities at Camp Pinerock, but it declines to host groups that teach theologies contrary to Christianity. Corporate, educational, and individual retreats are welcome. It's also a great place for a family reunion.

The camp, purchased in 1944 long before the edge of Prescott crept nearby, now has town conveniences within easy reach. Groups often combine activities at the camp's ropes course one day with bowling or miniature golf in town the next day.

The camp is open year-round and the pace slows only in December. Children's camp programs rule throughout the summer. A playground in a grassy park area marks the center of the camp for the younger ones.

Location: Prescott.
Description: A Nazarene church camp for adults and children.
How to get there: From AZ 89/Montezuma Street in Prescott, go west on Copper Basin Road for 1 mile. Go left (south) on Hemlock Avenue and then go right (west) on Pine Drive. Pine Drive curves south and ends at the church camp entrance.

The ropes course attracts the teenagers. Other recreational activities include hiking and horseback riding.

Many Christian leaders say they first felt the call to Christian ministry at youth church camps, where they could think about God in an atmosphere without judgment. Here, no one cares if you wear hand-me-down jeans or those with a designer label, and no one cares what your parents do for a living. The focus is on God and how he cares for you, no matter what.

A study by the National Association of Evangelicals showed that for every person who becomes a Christian in a church setting, two will profess belief in Jesus at a church camp or retreat. Deep spiritual matters are easier to discuss around the dark edges of a campfire in a place where you feel connected to community. Friendships grow closer through a common bond of belief.

Camp Pinerock counts itself among few camps with double- and queen-size beds, so up to 50 couples can stay at once in the dormitory-style rooms. In some buildings, the restrooms are shared.

A little more than a decade ago, the camp added upgraded facilities for adults who prefer not to sleep in dorm rooms. The Fiesta Suites are clean, comfortable, motel-style rooms with double beds, a pullout couch, a nearly full-size kitchen, a full bath, and a fireplace—but no telephone or television. The kitchen is stocked with dishes and utensils, a coffeemaker, and a microwave. Individuals are welcome to reserve these rooms. Cabins are the camp's third lodging option. All the buildings are heated and insulated, and the roads are plowed for that rare occasion when 30 inches of snow fall.

The camp can accommodate groups ranging in size from 15 to 400. Costs vary depending on group size, length of stay, and activities. For a group of less than 50, a five-day dormitory stay costs $189 per person, including 15 meals. That same stay would be $289 in the Fiesta Suites, the nicest rooms on the property. Meeting room use is $100 per weekday and $150 for a weekend day.

Meals are served in the cafeteria, buffet style. For an additional $2 per person, per meal, table service can be added for banquets. The food is better than typical camp fare. In keeping with the evangelical denomination's teachings, alcohol and smoking are both prohibited on the property.

Worship services can be held in both the large indoor auditorium or the open-air tabernacle surrounded by pine trees. As a ministry of the Arizona/Southern Nevada District of the Church of the Nazarene, the camp has a simple mission: "To provide an opportunity for a life-changing experience with Jesus Christ to every person that comes on the grounds."

54. Western Spirit Enrichment Center

Prescott, AZ
(866) 663-7747
E-mail: info@westernspiritranch.com
www.westernspiritranch.com

*A*t Western Spirit Enrichment Center, husband-and-wife founders Marian Carol and Gary Lowry created a spiritually and physically safe space for guests to connect with Spirit and nature, a place to heal and to grow. Visitors from around the world return home with a clearer vision of their lives and their paths. From this tranquil place, they leave with the tools and the power to heal themselves, as well as with a greater spiritual awareness to apply to their everyday lives.

One retreatant described the place with the words, "open heart and loving, nonjudgmental spirit." Another shared a prayer inspired by a weeklong stay: "God, be in me. Work with me. Work through me. And guide me. Amen."

A week in the nonthreatening environment of Western Spirit is different for everyone. The basic philosophy is that each individual is on a personal spiritual journey. You will not be told what's right or wrong for you. Instead, through workshops and activities, through spending time alone and with others, you will discover your heart and connect with Spirit, with God.

The teachings focus on the inner God-Spirit and center on the universal principle that, says Marian Carol, "God is love and all humankind are connected and one." The teachings speak to people regardless of their faith or religious background.

The daily schedule is flexible and relaxed. You can choose to attend workshops or take various excursions to places such as the Grand Canyon or Native American sites, or you can spend time alone journaling, reading, resting, and meditating. The day might include a massage and a yoga class and end with a performance by a Native American flute player.

Undeveloped state land surrounds the 11-acre property, which boasts a meditation garden with flowers and local desert plants. The hot tub on the huge, west-facing wraparound deck makes a perfect place to watch the sun as it sets behind the mountains, and it's equally lovely for stargazing. Cattle and horses roam the land, along with antelope, deer, and other wildlife. Nature brings balance into our lives, recharges our energies, and gives us the gift of its creative power. Nature enhances spirituality and the connection with God.

You will learn to choose love instead of fear and you will discover how to listen to the angels. In fact, Marian and Gary named the mountain behind the property "Angel Mountain." Marian says that her intuitive and psychic gifts have manifested incredible experiences in her life,

Location: North of Prescott.
Description: A retreat center of self-discovery, healing, and growth guided by Spirit.
How to get there: Visitors must make arrangements in advance for the owners to pick them up in Prescott. You will not need a car during your visit. If you need to drive yourself to the property, please contact the owners for directions.

and she can help you develop your own intuitive powers as you know the God-Spirit within you.

The time here can be emotional as you open up your heart and allow wounds from the past to emerge. Releasing the hurt and replacing it with love is the first step of healing, embracing spiritual renewal, and recognizing true blessings. The goal is to teach retreatants to stop spending spiritual energy pushing down the pain and avoiding the hurt when they could use that energy to manifest their hearts' desires with God's help.

Complete with candles and fresh flowers, the two large, Western-style guest rooms have mini-refrigerators, hair dryers, and bathrooms. Stays are Sunday through Saturday and begin at about $1,200 per person for double occupancy. The rate includes meals, workshops, and all excursions except skiing. Meals can be adjusted according to the tastes of the guests, and arrangements can be made to meet the needs of vegetarians and those with food allergies.

55. Living Water Worship & Teaching Center

595 Aspaas Rd.　　　　　**Mailing address:**
Cornville, AZ 86325　　　P.O. Box 529
(928) 634-4421　　　　　Cornville, AZ 86325

*A*t home, the interruptions are constant. The telephone rings. The kids want something. There's another meeting and you have to work overtime to meet the next deadline.

Jesus, the living water for whom this conference center was named, got away from the crowd to pray and spend time with his Father. The Living Water Worship & Teaching Center opened in 1981 to provide Christians with a place to follow Jesus' example and let the Holy Spirit minister to their needs.

It's easier to get in touch with your spiritual side in a 25-acre green oasis in the desert with a pond, horse pasture, and benches lining Oak Creek. Here, you will find time to read and listen to God—away from the complications of 21st-century living. You'll find inspiration in the words of the prophet Isaiah:

> The wilderness and the dry land shall be glad, the desert shall rejoice and blossom….They shall see the glory of the Lord, the majesty of our God….Everlasting joy shall be upon their heads; they shall obtain joy and gladness, and sorrow and sighing shall flee away.

The prayer chapel and prayer garden are available anytime, day or night. A communion service takes place at 10 a.m. Fridays in the prayer chapel.

Location: Cornville.

Description: A Christian retreat center on a lake with both dormitory- and hotel-style accommodations.

How to get there: From I-17, take County Road 119 (Exit 293, marked Cornville/Lake Montezuma/McGuireville) northwest about 8.5 miles. At Aspaas Road (the first road past Casey's Corner) go right (north). Aspaas Road ends at the retreat center about 1 mile down the road, which includes two sharp turns.

Soft, inspirational music plays in the rooms, but you can turn it off. The rooms have no phones or televisions. The living room of the main chapel building houses a library that is available only to those on a personal retreat.

The facilities are right for one person or a group up to 125. The center does not charge extra for meeting rooms. A two-night group retreat costs about $86 to $108 per person, with five meals included. Personal retreats including three meals cost about $65 a night for one person and $110 a night for a couple. The center provides bedding and towels. Children are allowed (but not babies), although the center is not necessarily set up to entertain them. Alcoholic beverages, nonprescription drugs, and firearms are not permitted on the property. Smoking is prohibited inside the buildings, but is acceptable outside.

The dormitory-style rooms have bunk beds and shared bathrooms. The hotel-style rooms in the Gethsemane Retreat House were designed especially for personal retreats. Each room has a recliner, a writing desk, two single beds, a bathroom, and a private patio overlooking the grounds. Some rooms are wheelchair accessible.

Meals are served in the dining room, which also provides coffee, drinks, and snacks throughout the day. Individuals on personal retreats may pick up their meals and eat on the patio off their rooms, but groups cannot. The kitchen staff makes homemade meals, including desserts and fresh-baked bread, and can address special dietary needs.

Groups provide their own retreat programs and individuals will be left alone. Group retreats book well in advance, but individual retreats typically can be planned with less notice. If you're not quite sure how to go about planning a private or group retreat, the Living Water staff provides a retreat book based on its experience with coordinating retreats for more than 50,000 people. The book walks you through each step needed for a successful retreat.

56. Garchen Buddhist Institute

P.O. Box 4318
Chino Valley, AZ 86323
(928) 925-5847
E-mail: garchen@garchen.com
www.garchen.com

*A*ll over the Garchen Buddhist Institute's 75-acre property hang colorful Tibetan prayer flags in blue, yellow, green, red, and white, a bright contrast to the surrounding greens and reddish-browns of Prescott National Forest. The Tibetan word for prayer flags loosely translates to "wind horse." The concept behind the flags is that everything is connected to everything else: The sun shines on the flags and the wind blows them, carrying the prayers outward to the rest of the world. No matter how tattered, the flags endure, strung from tree to tree, along buildings, and on poles. The prayers written on the flags say different blessings, wishing for happiness and freedom from suffering for all beings.

The Garchen Buddhist Institute hosted its first programs in January 2000. Buddhist teachings are designed to bring forth compassion, loving kindness, and patience in your conduct toward yourself and others. The historical Buddha, through meditation and investigation, discovered the source of sufferings. Through practices of meditation and study, suffering decreases while happiness and wisdom increase.

The teachings of Buddhism allow people to weather adversity successfully. The Buddha said enlightenment has 180,000 different paths, all of them perfect and complete, because there are that many different kinds of people. If you have an affinity with and devotion to a certain path, then that way is for you.

The institute's founder is His Eminence Garchen Rinpoche, a Drikung Kagyu lama who was known in the 13th century as the Siddha Gar Chodingpa, a heart disciple of the founder of the Drikung Kagyu lineage of Tibetan Buddhism. In ancient India, he had incarnated as Mahasiddha Aryadeva, the lotus-born disciple of the great Nagarjuna. Garchen Rinpoche was recognized and enthroned in eastern Tibet at the age of 7.

During China's Cultural Revolution, the 22-year-old was incarcerated. He spent 20 years in prison, where he practiced secretly and attained the lama's wisdom mind. Since his release in 1979, he has founded the Garchen

Location: 10 miles northeast of Chino Valley.

Description: A Tibetan Buddhist center of teaching and meditation.

How to get there: The institute is off a dirt road out of Chino Valley. Visitors are asked to call ahead for directions.

Buddhist Institute and he has worked to rebuild the Drikung Kagyu monasteries and re-establish Buddhist teachings in eastern Tibet.

The buildings on the institute's property are of smooth stucco, the same color as the ground, and the green tile roofs draw their color from the surrounding trees and shrubs. The dining room has deep porches surrounding it, showing off uninterrupted views of the valleys and mountains.

In the larger of two temples, Tibetan carpets decorated with flowers stretch across the wooden floor. This temple is typically used for group teachings and practice. The stupa—a smaller temple for practice and individual prayer—has a sand mandala and, written in calligraphy on each of the eight walls, the eight essential teachings of Buddha. One reads, "Commit no non-virtuous deed. All virtuous deeds do in perfection. Completely tame your mind. This is the teaching of the Buddha."

On Sundays from 9 a.m. to noon, the center hosts public practice in the temple, but you must call ahead. Individual practice is available by appointment. Everyone is asked to remove their shoes before entering the temples.

Throughout the year, numerous retreat and teaching programs feature teachers from around the world. Both qualified practitioners and those seeking time away attend the retreats. During teachings and retreats, you are asked to use fragrance-free products out of respect for those with asthma and allergies.

The center's two guesthouses are inexpensive to rent. One guesthouse has a kitchenette, a living room, and two bedrooms, each with an attached bathroom and a private entry. The other has five rooms that share two baths, a living room, and a kitchenette. Whether prepared in the guesthouse kitchenettes or served in the dining room, the food here is strictly vegetarian. Larger groups often camp or rent hotel rooms in town.

The institute also is open for weddings, ceremonies, and workshops that fit the center's philosophy. A nonviolent communications workshop was among the first outside programs to take place here. The property also has a bookstore featuring goods from Tibet.

Sacred Places

57. Montezuma Well

Montezuma Castle National Monument
527 Main St.
Camp Verde, AZ 86322
(928) 567-3322
E-mail: MOCA_Administration@nps.gov
www.nps.gov/moca/home.htm

Mailing address:
P.O. Box 219
Camp Verde, AZ 86322

*M*ore than a million people visit Montezuma Castle National Monument each year to view one of the best-preserved cliff dwellings in the United States. But 11 miles northeast of the busy national monument lies the more sacred site, a natural sinkhole in limestone where Native Americans still come to pray and to draw water for ceremonies.

The well, which measures nearly 400 feet across and 55 feet deep, formed when the dome of an ancient subterranean cavern collapsed and flooded. The water's temperature stays an even 76 degrees year-round—too warm for fish, although the well nurtures a few forms of plant and animal life found nowhere else the world.

The sinkhole is the sacred place of creation for both the Yavapai and Apache nations, according to the tribes. They tell that their ancestors came

Location: North of Camp Verde.

Description: A limestone sinkhole connected with a Native American creation story.

How to get there: From I-17, go east on County Road 119 (Exit 293, marked Cornville/Lake Montezuma/McGuireville). About 0.25 mile past McGuireville, go left (northeast) on Beaver Creek Road. Follow the signs for about 4 miles to the turnoff for the parking lot. Go right and continue to the parking lot at the end of the 0.3-mile road.

from the underworld through the sinkhole and lived there. When the hole flooded, one of them went over the edge and was saved to start a new tribe.

A million and a half gallons of water a day flow up from the underground springs and out through an opening in the side, cut by the ancient people who lived there between A.D. 900 and 1400. The Sinaguans built an elaborate irrigation system using water from the well for their crops. This water supported a large and widespread society.

Standing at the edge of the well, you can imagine a green and busy valley stretching out for miles. A short but steep hiking trail takes you down to where the water flows through the small, cavelike opening along the shady banks. You also can walk the opposite way around the well and down another steep hiking trail to the other side of the outlet, where you can touch the dark, bluish-green water as its flows in the narrow channel. There, the cliffs shelter benches from the strong winds.

The signs invite you to experience the sacred nature of the water: "Take the time to see the sky. Find shapes in the clouds. Hear the murmur of the wind and touch the cool water. Walk softly. We are the intruders, tolerated briefly by an infinite universe."

Ancient Aztec emperor Montezuma never actually visited the site, though early settlers lent it his name. He lived several centuries earlier, 2,000 miles to the south.

You must pay a small entrance fee to access Montezuma Castle National Monument, but visits to Montezuma Well are free of charge. Hours for the monument and well are 8 a.m. to 5 p.m. daily. Montezuma Castle was set aside as a national monument in 1906 and has been maintained by the National Park Service since 1947.

For a tour with a Native American guide, contact Native Visions at (928) 567-3035. Tours start at $20 per person for Montezuma Castle or Montezuma Well, and a combo tour is $35 per person.

58. Tuzigoot National Monument

P.O. Box 219
Camp Verde, AZ 86322
(928) 634-5564
www.nps.gov/tuzi/home.htm

At many Native American ruin sites, you can only observe from a distance. At Tuzigoot National Monument, you can walk right up and into the pueblo built between A.D. 1125 and 1400 by the Sinaguans, an ancient people who inhabited the valley of the Verde River.

Tuzigoot is one of the Verde Valley's 50 major pueblo sites. In 1939, President Franklin D. Roosevelt granted national monument status to Tuzigoot, a site that had been excavated by the federal government's Civil Works Administration.

Location: Near Clarkdale.

Description: An excavated Sinaguan pueblo, one of 50 major pueblo sites in the Verde Valley.

How to get there: The entrance to the national monument is off AZ 89A, north of Clarkdale.

The pueblo perches on a ridge 120 feet above the valley, with long views all around. The Sinaguans built the pueblo during a period of 400 years. At its largest, the pueblo had 86 ground-floor rooms and 15 second-story rooms. As many as 225 people might have lived there during its peak. Using ladders, they entered the pueblo through openings in the roofs.

The visitors' center gives you details about their everyday lives. Tuzigoot has two 0.25-mile trails and offers guided tours daily. The visitors' center and the Tavasci Marsh Overlook Trail are wheelchair accessible, but wheelchairs and baby strollers are not recommended on the Ruins Trail even though it is paved. Visitors are asked to keep to the trails, leash their pets, and refrain from climbing or sitting on the walls. The entry fee is $3, and children 16 and younger are admitted free. The site is open from 8 a.m. to 5 p.m., with extended hours until 7 p.m. in the summer. It is closed on Christmas Day.

59. El Dorado Hot Spring

P.O. Box 10
Tonopah, AZ 85354
(623) 386-5412
E-mail: hotspring@el-dorado.com
www.el-dorado.com

*N*o wonder the catchphrase for El Dorado Hot Spring is "a million miles from Monday." You might forget about returning to work altogether after a day at this relaxing, rustic spa, with its natural subterranean spring of hot mineral water.

Arizona has hundreds of naturally occurring hot springs, but most are reached only after long hikes. This is one of the few in the state accessible from a paved road.

El Dorado's owners explain that according to Native American belief, hot springs are sacred places of emergence from Mother Earth. The vent, or "sipapu," allowed creatures from other worlds to surface on this plane. Although all nature is treated with reverence, hot springs were considered sacred, healing places.

Location: Tonopah, about 40 miles west of Phoenix.
Description: A rustic, healing hot spring in the desert.
How to get there: From I-10, exit at Tonopah (Exit 94). Go south on 411th Avenue and turn right (west) on Indian School Road. El Dorado is 0.25 mile farther on the south side of the road.

The 6.7-acre property has five private areas with two soaking tanks each, and one semiprivate space with six tanks. The water temperature stays around 112 to 114 degrees. Shades and mist machines, along with cool water to adjust the temperature of the soak, make summer days more comfortable. At night, it's cooler and the stars pop out in the darkened sky, away from the lighted cities.

"Sunset" is the most popular private soaking area. The large, main soaking tank is made of stones and the water comes out through a geode. The area has an unobstructed view of Saddle Mountain, which evokes positive energy.

At hot springs, private areas tend to be clothing optional, meaning you can soak while wearing a bathing suit or nothing at all. The owners of El Dorado, Camilla Van Sickle and Bill Pennington, belong to the Naturist Society and are contributors to *Nude & Natural* magazine, as well as *Hot Springs & Hot Pools of the Southwest* by Marjorie Gersh-Young (Aqua Thermal Access, 2001). The Naturist Society promotes "wholesome, non-sexual nude recreation" and "clothing-optional lifestyles." At El Dorado, some people come to always soak in the nude. Others get private spaces and still wear bathing suits.

Clothing is not allowed at El Dorado's "Desert Pete," the communal soaking area, which has three soaking tubs, a 10-foot cement tub, and two 6-foot galvanized steel tubs. In the common area, clothing is optional, so don't be surprised when you see people walking around in the nude, a towel over a shoulder and nothing else.

After spending years traveling and living out of their RV, Van Sickle and Pennington found the property in 1996 and opened El Dorado in 1997. Although Tonopah once was home to seven or so hot springs operations, this property was not among them. Van Sickle and Pennington wanted to start from scratch in an area free of other people's energies, they say.

Properties of water differ among hot springs. The water here, pumped from the ground, is drinkable and has a pH of 8.3. The minerals and the heat soothe aching muscles and the water's properties leave your skin feeling as smooth as silk.

Bamboo watered by the hot springs grows here and the tanks at one private area overlook a fish pond with lily pads. The property's stone meditation circle is a place to focus and connect with the divine in a natural desert setting; guests are asked to wear clothes there.

Although not a campground, El Dorado Hot Spring welcomes overnight guests for extended soaks. The property has a one-room cabin, the Motel California, with a bathroom and provided sheets and towels. The cost is about $40 per person and $55 per couple. Private soaks start at $7.50 an hour.

January through March is the high season here, although people visit year-round. The place doesn't feel crowded, even if all the spaces are occupied. You can make reservations for your soak in advance or just show up. Hours are 9 a.m. to 9 p.m. daily. No pets are allowed, and alcohol and smoking are permitted in private areas only, not in common areas. El Dorado also offers massage therapy and reflexology, along with other treatments.

60. Painted Rocks Petroglyph Site

Painted Rock Dam Road

Mailing address:
Bureau of Land Management
Phoenix Field Office
21605 N. Seventh Ave.
Phoenix, AZ 85027
(602) 580-5500
www.az.blm.gov/pfo/paint.htm

Past the agricultural fields that give way to open desert, far from houses and businesses, a large pile of rocks bears hundreds of petroglyphs likely fashioned by the Hohokam between 300 and 1450 A.D. Painted Rocks Petroglyph Site gives you an up-close look at the extensive petroglyphs in relative solitude. Although it boasts some amenities, the site is somewhat off the beaten path.

No one really knows what these petroglyphs pecked into the rocks symbolize, but archaeologists and modern Native Americans have theories. Petroglyphs could have connected the ancient people with the spirit world. The animal figures, called zoomorphs, could be clan symbols or an exercise in magic to bring good hunting. Anthropomorphs are figures that look like humans. The concentric circles could have symbolized a passageway from one world to another, a way for the shaman or medicine man to go from the spiritual to the material world.

Early Catholic missionaries might have left their own symbols behind. An outlined cross could represent the planet Venus or a star, but it also is a symbol of Quetzalcoatl, a deity in Mexico who became an astral figure. The site is along the Juan Bautista de Anza Historic Trail, where the explorer of the same name passed through in 1775. He noted the petroglyphs in his journal.

Location: About 14 miles west of Gila Bend.
Description: An extensive petroglyph site.
How to get there: From I-8, take Painted Rock Dam Road (Exit 102) north. Go about 11 miles on the paved road. At the curve, go straight (west) on the good dirt Rocky Point Road for about 0.5 mile to the parking lot.

Feel the sacred presence here, but remember not to touch or climb on the rocks to avoid damaging the petroglyphs. Rattlesnakes and other poisonous creatures make their homes here, so watch where you place your hands and feet.

The site has bathrooms, picnic ramadas, and grills but no water. Visitors' fees are not charged May 1 to September 30, mainly because with summer temperatures topping 120 degrees, it's too hot to visit the site comfortably. The rest of the year, the fee is $2 per vehicle. Camping is $4 per vehicle, per night, and the site is always open.

Region Four
Grand Canyon and
Northern Arizona

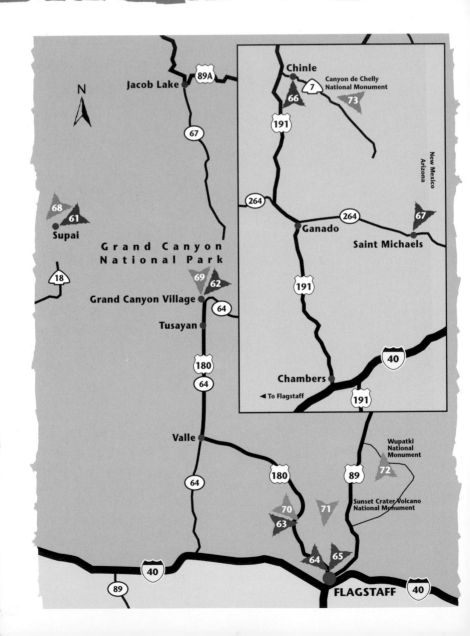

*F*rom the Grand Canyon to Canyon de Chelly, northern Arizona's natural wonders amaze. Along with the area's wide swathes of beautiful scenery come unique spiritual experiences and opportunities for worship.

You cannot stand at the rim of the Grand Canyon without catching your breath as the views stretch miles before you and a mile below you. Inside the canyon, near the small village of Supai, three legendary turquoise waterfalls mark a sacred place of beauty. The village houses the only church located within the Grand Canyon, Havasupai Bible Church, where campers join local tribal members for worship each Sunday.

In Saint Michaels, a saint walked the grounds of St. Michael's mission and school. A museum at the facility now honors the contributions of St. Katharine Drexel, only the second American to be canonized by the Roman Catholic Church. Another Catholic church, Our Lady of Fatima in Chinle, blends Navajo and Christian beliefs. Here, parishioners praise God but also realize that God was at work long before the Catholic missionaries arrived over a century ago.

As the hub for local Bahá'ís, Macy's Coffee House & European Bakery in Flagstaff serves up terrific drinks along with the spirit of the unity of humankind. In the shadow of the San Francisco Peaks north of Flagstaff live the sacred white buffalo believed to be the fulfillment of a Lakota prophecy. Nearby, you'll also discover a tiny roadside chapel where people stop to post written prayers all over the walls. If God has a mailbox, it's here at the Chapel of the Holy Dove.

Unlike other parts of the state, northern Arizona offers no retreat centers that serve the general public. The winters are cold and the smaller towns are more remote. Consider the trip to Supai, nestled at the bottom of the Grand Canyon: After about a six-hour drive from Phoenix, you must hike, ride a horse, or take a helicopter to the village. But, for an unmatched experience to inspire you to the depths of your soul, every place listed here is worth the travel time.

Sanctuaries

61. Havasupai Bible Church

P.O. Box 39
Supai, AZ 86435
(928) 448-2651

The only church in the bottom of the Grand Canyon draws as many campers and hikers as locals. Inside the tiny town of Supai, with sheer rock walls rising all around, the Havasupai Bible Church gives glory to God in a converted Quonset hut. The church is near the middle of the village, noticeable by its cross and bell out front.

Location: The village of Supai at the bottom of the Grand Canyon.
Description: The only church inside the Grand Canyon.
How to get there: You can hike or ride a horse 8 miles into Supai or take the helicopter, which typically runs three or four days a week. The trailhead is at Hualapai Hilltop, off a paved road. From Route 66 (AZ 66), take Indian Route 18 northeast for about 60 miles to the parking lot at Hualapai Hilltop. The turnoff to Indian Route 18 is about 30 miles west of Seligman on Route 66. Entry and camping permits are required. For specific details on travel, call the Havasupai Tourist Office at (928) 448-2120 or visit the website at www.havasupaitribe.com.

The bell rings on Sundays, announcing services. Hikers and campers often come dressed in shorts, T-shirts, and hiking boots. Inside the sanctuary are metal chairs, a concrete floor, and a picture of Jesus—and the love of Christ all around. The independent church is Bible-believing and Bible-preaching.

Around 1945, Episcopalians established the church in a Quonset hut left behind from another project. In the mid-1950s, a missionary from the United Indian Mission (UIM) hiked into Supai. The tribal chairman heard the message and asked for the UIM to send missionaries down.

Today, the church is led by a member of the tribe who conducts services in English and sometimes in Havasupai, the language of the 600-member Havasupai Tribe. Children's classes take place at 9:30 a.m. and services are at 11 a.m. on Sundays.

The church enjoys breathtaking natural surroundings in one of Arizona's most scenic spots. Its modest material makeup seems grander when you consider that everything that comes into Supai must arrive by helicopter, or be carried by horses or people over 8 miles of moderately difficult terrain.

62. Shrine of the Ages

Grand Canyon National Park
P.O. Box 129
Grand Canyon, AZ 86023
(928) 638-7888
www.nps.gov/grca

Built of rock and wood, the Shrine of the Ages blends with the surrounding pine trees. Rather than having windows of stained glass, this building's windows open to views of God's awesome creation.

Grand Canyon visitors and park employees alike come to Shrine of the Ages, a place for multiple denominations to worship. The facility also serves as a community center for park service talks.

Location: South Rim of Grand Canyon National Park.

Description: A church building used by multiple groups for worship and a variety of park programs.

How to get there: The South Rim is 80 miles north of Flagstaff. Take US 180 northwest to AZ 64. Turn right (north) and continue through Tusayan to the south entrance of Grand Canyon National Park. Shrine of the Ages is west of Parking Lot A, which is past Mather Point.

If you would like to incorporate worship into your Grand Canyon trip, the best way to find out about the various church services is to call the different denominational offices, as service times and programs vary throughout the year. Here are the numbers: Church of Jesus Christ of Latter-day Saints, (928) 638-4050; Grand Canyon Assembly of God, (928) 638-9415; Grand Canyon Baptist Church, (928) 638-2790; Grand Canyon Community Church, (928) 638-2340; Jehovah's Witnesses, (928) 635-0070; Roman Catholic, (928) 638-2390. Current schedules also are posted at Shrine of the Ages, at Mather Campground, and at the information kiosk near the post office. The National Park Service does not endorse or sponsor religious services.

The South Rim is open 24 hours a day, 365 days a year. The entry fee per vehicle is $20 for a pass good for seven days.

63. Chapel of the Holy Dove

US 180, near milepost 236 north of Flagstaff

The Chapel of the Holy Dove is a place of prayer like no other. People don't just stop to pray in the tiny, A-frame chapel with windows showcasing the San Francisco Peaks. They leave behind their requests on paper in a rainbow of colors and myriad sizes.

Pieces of paper cover the walls, attached with tape, glue, staples—whatever a body can find. More notes are anchored with pebbles to keep them from blowing away in the strong wind. When the door opens and the wind blows through, all those notes flap like the wings of a flock of doves, the only sound in the quiet meadow.

If God has a mailbox, this is where you will find it. One message says, "Dear God, take care of Vernon through his surgery today. [Signed,] his sister." And another: "Dear God, thanks for letting us be able to find this place and have such beauty around us. Your grace is forever in my heart. Without you, dear God, we would not be together today. Bless our children and family and everyone who touches us."

Location: About 20 miles north of Flagstaff.

Description: A small, roadside, nondenominational chapel filled with written prayers.

How to get there: From Flagstaff, go north on US 180. The chapel will be on the right side of the road before milepost 236.

People also leave behind rosaries, crucifixes, and scripture verses. On a sticky note on the small wooden pulpit, someone wrote a verse inspired by the view: "Psalms 121: I lift up my eyes to the hills. Where does my help come from? My help comes from the Lord, our maker of heaven and earth. Trust in our Lord Jesus Christ."

With a floor of loose pebbles, the simple chapel looks bigger on the inside than from the outside. Six benches face the pulpit, windows, a stone altar, and a cross.

The chapel is a popular spot for weddings, but there's no office to contact or number to call for reservations. What do you do? You write a note asking all who come to the chapel to reserve the time and day for a wedding and leave your request somewhere on the walls.

64. Nativity of the Blessed Virgin Mary Chapel

16 W. Cherry Ave.
Flagstaff, AZ 86001
(928) 779-1341

Mailing address:
San Francisco de Asis Parish
P.O. Box 1946
Flagstaff, AZ 86002

E-mail: san_francisco@diocesephoenix.org
www.diocesephoenix.org/parish/sf_fran_assisi

From the edges of the roof, gargoyle statues watch over the Nativity of the Blessed Virgin Mary Chapel in Flagstaff. This historic Gothic-style church was dedicated in 1930 as the congregation's third home. Parishioners helped build the church by collecting wagonloads of the native volcanic rock, called malpais. They purposely selected rocks covered with lichen, which still grows today on the church's walls and gives a softer edge to the rough, dark rocks.

Michael Riordan, one of the Riordan brothers important in Flagstaff's early days for owning the Arizona Lumber and Timber Company, spurred the construction of Nativity of the Blessed Virgin Mary Chapel. He wrote that the architect should "produce a rugged, fortress-like structure with deep shadows that would fit in and be part of the bold mountain background, while embellishing it at the same time with the lightness of contrasting color and the effect of airiness produced by long lines, slender windows and deep splays and the remarkable, noble tower."

It was a difficult mission, to be sure, but one that architect Emmet Martin accomplished. The church stands as a testament to the faith of early Flagstaff Catholics and serves as a place to worship and build faith today.

Parishioners dedicated the original Church of the Nativity on Christmas Day 1888, making it the first Catholic church in Flagstaff and the first church along the railway line. A traveling priest had conducted Mass in homes and other locales until then.

This first church was located in south Flagstaff, but by 1911, the congregation had moved because the Catholic community wanted to be closer to its school and convent. Eventually, the parish desired a larger church, so the Nativity of the Blessed Virgin Mary Chapel was built in its current location half a block away.

The original church's name came from its first Mass, held on Christmas Day. Some people mistakenly think the church's name still makes reference to the Nativity of Christ, but it actually refers to the birth of the Blessed Virgin Mary. In an alcove behind the altar, a mural depicts the scene of Mary's birth, with St. Anne tenderly holding the newborn Mary. Mary's father, St. Joachim, and other family members welcome the future Mother of God as angels surround the adoring group. Stephen Juharos, a Hungarian-born artist who lives in Sedona, painted the mural. Although the alcove appears to have been created specifically for the mural, the inspirational artwork did not grace the space until 1979, when Arizona pioneer and longtime church member Viola Babbitt raised the money for the mural and commissioned Juharos to paint it.

English-language Mass takes place at 8 a.m. Sunday, with another Mass following at 10 a.m. in Spanish. Weekday Masses commence at 12:15 p.m.

65. Bahá'í Faith

Macy's European Coffee House & Bakery
14 S. Beaver St.
Flagstaff, AZ 86001
(928) 774-2243
E-mail: macyscoffee@earthlink.net

Macy's European Coffee House & Bakery involves much more than wonderful coffee, although the brew here ranks among the best. Owner and founder Tim Macy started the coffeehouse in 1980 as a business based on his personal and spiritual beliefs as a Bahá'í.

On the walls, sharing space with a sign featuring the coffee of the day, hangs a picture of the religion's 19th-century founder, Bahá'u'lláh. Also posted there are some of his quotes: "The Earth is but one country and mankind its citizens," and "Ye are all leaves of one tree and the fruits of one branch." Bahá'ís believe in progressive revelation and that Bahá'u'lláh, who was born in Persia and lived between 1817 and 1892, was the last messenger of God. They also recognize Abraham, Moses, Krishna, Buddha, Zoroaster, Christ, and Mohammed as messengers of God.

At 7 p.m. on the first Friday of each month, the Bahá'ís meet at Macy's—and there's always free coffee. The place serves as the spiritual hub for the Bahá'ís in Flagstaff because they do not have a center dedicated solely to worship. When they're not convening at Macy's, they meet in each other's homes.

Everyone is accepted in a spirit of unity. "The most important thing here is the love," says Tim Macy. "People feel the spirit of this place. It's so blessed." He jokes that he's no businessman, so the coffeehouse *has* to be blessed to have kept its doors open for 23 years.

Macy's hours are 6 a.m. to 8 p.m. Sunday through Wednesday, and 7 a.m. to 10 p.m. Thursday through Saturday. The coffeehouse offers an all-vegetarian menu with bakery selections that include wheat-free, dairy-free, and vegan options. This establishment also presents live music to underscore its Bohemian, counterculture atmosphere.

Bahá'ís number about five million worldwide in more than 200 countries. They believe in the oneness of God, the oneness of religion, and the oneness of humanity. The central teachings of the religion are that humanity is a single race and the time has come for society's unification, breaking down barriers of race, class, creed, and country. They support a peaceful, global society free from prejudice; the full equality of men and women; the unity and relativity of all religious truth; and the elimination of extremes in poverty and wealth. To learn more about the Bahá'í Faith, visit www.bahai.org.

Location: Downtown Flagstaff.
Description: A coffeehouse that serves as the hub for the Bahá'í community in Flagstaff.
How to get there: From Route 66 (Business I-40) in Flagstaff, go south on Beaver Street. The coffeehouse is two blocks south of the train station.

66. Our Lady of Fatima Catholic Church

P.O. Box 2119
Chinle, AZ 86503
(928) 674-5413

Set apart from a world of religions that often seek to displace other beliefs, Our Lady of Fatima Catholic Church honors both Christianity and the traditional spirituality of the Navajo. Mass begins with the blessing of the four directions in English. The prayer closes with the words, "Let us always walk in beauty, walk in beauty, walk in beauty." The priest wafts cedar smoke with an eagle feather and blesses the people. In the traditional Navajo way of a blessing, worshipers draw the smoke close to their faces and breathe deeply. They kneel and pray before the Eucharist as they repeat, "Jesus Christ has died for us and has risen from the tomb."

The church is shaped like a traditional hogan, with a skyhole in the top of the building and a 6-foot hole cut in the concrete floor to expose the sacred earth. The hole reminds people of the Navajo creation story, in which all forms of life came into this present world through an emergence hole. Baptisms are performed in a pottery baptismal font that sits on a stump in the hole, with the water from the pitcher pouring down and returning to the earth as a symbol of the new life found in Christ. Four stages of life are depicted in images on the baptismal font: a baby on a cradleboard, a young lady awaiting the future, a woman weaving a rug, and an elderly man sitting on a horse and watching sheep.

Paintings of the four mountains sacred to the Navajo hang on the north, south, east, and west walls. White deerskin, used by medicine men, drapes across the altar table. Images of Yeis, the holy people of the Navajo, are etched into the glass entry doors as a reminder that people should walk a holy path. A red and blue rainbow painted on the wall depicts the native path of peace and harmony. The rainbow arcs over the Stations of the Cross, which illustrate Jesus' journey to the cross.

The church is a place where the Navajo can feel comfortable worshiping without abandoning their traditions. Some churches teach that if it's not in the Bible, it's wrong, says the priest, the Rev. Blane Grein. But Our Lady of Fatima's members appreciate the merging of the faiths and believe that God was at work long before the Catholic church came here. Prayers, the parishioners say, all go to the same God.

Franciscan priests arrived in Chinle in the late 1890s. They established a church in 1905 in an adobe structure, which served its purpose until a traditional stone church was built. In 1960, the church moved to a new building. By the 1980s, it needed expensive repairs, so the parish and the Diocese of Gallup decided to build a new one instead.

By then, the pope and the American bishops were encouraging parishes to embrace, not replace, various cultures where they were spreading the gospel. This was the perfect opportunity to reflect and affirm Navajo culture, so the Navajo church members planned everything. The first Mass was held in the church's new home on Christmas 1989.

In Navajo belief, rocks are placed atop one another as a symbol of prayer, called a prayer pile. In Our Lady of Fatima, the table on which the Eucharist sits is a kind of prayer pile. When the church building was under construction, members brought in prayers written on pieces of paper. Within the prayer pile table of cement and petrified rock, those prayers act as perpetual petitions. The tabernacle, a container built to resemble a Navajo summer home, sits atop the table and houses the Eucharist.

Attendance averages from 100 to 200 people at weekend Masses, which start at 7:30 p.m. on Saturday and 9 a.m. on Sunday. After Sunday Mass, the congregation meets in the parish hall for coffee and doughnuts.

Location: Chinle, on the Navajo Indian Reservation.
Description: A Catholic church that blends traditional Navajo beliefs into its worship services and church design.
How to get there: From I-40 at Chambers, go north on US 191 (Exit 333) about 80 miles to Indian Route 7. Go right (east) and follow the signs into Chinle, about 2 miles. The church is on Indian Route 7, the main route through town, just before the gas station.

67. St. Michael's School, Mission, and Museum

24 Mission Rd.
Saint Michaels, AZ 86511
(928) 871-4171
E-mail: stmikesofm@aol.com

Mailing address:
P.O. Box 680
Saint Michaels, AZ 86511

On these grounds walked St. Katharine Drexel, the second American canonized by the Roman Catholic Church. After her death in 1955, she was credited with restoring hearing to two deaf children. These miracles opened the way for her to be declared a saint on October 1, 2000, by Pope John Paul II.

The daughter of wealthy Philadelphia financier Francis Drexel, St. Katharine spent her fortune (worth about $250 million today) establishing schools and churches for African-Americans and Native Americans. During her lifetime, she opened, staffed, and supported almost 60 missions and schools throughout the country. She founded a new order in Pennsylvania—the Sisters of the Blessed Sacrament—as well as Xavier University in New Orleans. The country's first African-American college, Xavier University has been the only both Black and Catholic institute of higher learning in the United States since 1925.

But before then, in 1902, St. Katharine founded St. Michael's mission and school near Window Rock on the Navajo Reservation. The school goes from kindergarten to 12th grade. National statistics show that about 9 percent of Native Americans go to college after high school graduation. St. Michael's graduates enter college at a rate of 90 percent.

Location: Saint Michaels, 3 miles west of the Arizona–New Mexico border.

Description: A Catholic church, school, and museum affiliated with St. Katharine Drexel, the second American to be canonized.

How to get there: From the intersection of AZ 264 and Mission Road, go south at the post office.

The original mission, the smaller building next to the church and school, now houses a museum. This building of beauty and strength served its initial purpose well, as all children deserve the best, St. Katharine said. The museum's displays educate visitors on the early Franciscans at the school and mission, and on the life of St. Katharine. The museum is open on weekdays from 9 a.m. to 5 p.m. between Memorial Day and Labor Day, with additional weekend hours added periodically. Mass is held regularly at the church; please call ahead for the current schedule.

Also of interest, St. Joan of Arc Catholic Church in Phoenix has installed a side altar that was used by St. Katharine in her home and in the chapel at Sisters of the Blessed Sacrament convent. She may have received her vocation to become a nun through prayer at the altar. The 12-foot high, hand-carved, solid walnut altar is considered a second-class relic because she used it. The church is located at 3801 E. Greenway Rd. in Phoenix, and the phone number is (602) 867-9171.

Sacred Places

68. Havasu Falls

Havasupai Tourist Office
P.O. Box 160
Supai, AZ 86435
(928) 448-2120
E-mail: touristoffice@havasupaitribe.com
www.havasupaitribe.com

*H*avasu Falls might be Arizona's most scenic and most hidden spot. The blue-green water gives the Havasupai Tribe its name: "ha" meaning water, "vasu" meaning blue-green, and "pai" meaning people.

In tribal beliefs, spirits gather at sacred Havasu Falls. But no matter what your creed, this amazing place will inspire you—whether it's the cool water's unearthly color or its sound roaring in your ears. Floods in 1997 destroyed the oft-photographed travertine pools, but limestone deposits in the water slowly will rebuild them. If you witnessed Havasu Falls before the floods, you will know what you're missing. Nevertheless, the beauty of the scene still strikes awe.

Because the village of Supai is at the bottom of the Grand Canyon, the trip there is difficult. You can only reach it by hiking, riding on horseback, or taking a helicopter. The falls is another 2-mile hike from the village.

Hiking trails and campgrounds link Havasu Falls, Navajo Falls, and Mooney Falls, the latter of which plunges farther than Niagara Falls. Summer temperatures here range from the 60s to the upper 90s, deeming the 70-degree water a refreshing way to cool down. In winter, the season that draws the fewest visitors, temperatures dip down into the 20s.

Historically, the Havasupai people roamed northern Arizona. They lived in the canyon in summer, and in winter they moved to places with more abundant food and firewood. As Anglo settlers encroached on tribal lands, the Havasupai were pushed into the canyon permanently.

Of the tribe's approximately 650 members, about 450 live in the village of Supai—a stretch of houses (some with satellite dishes), a lodge, a post office, a restaurant, a church, and a general store. Tourism serves as the tribe's main source of income today.

Location: The bottom of the Grand Canyon.
Description: Beautiful blue-green falls sacred to the Havasupai Tribe.
How to get there: You can hike or ride a horse 8 miles to the falls or take the helicopter into Supai, which typically runs three or four days a week, and then hike another 2 miles to the falls. The trailhead is at Hualapai Hilltop, off a paved road. From Route 66 (AZ 66), take Indian Route 18 northeast for about 60 miles to the parking lot at Hualapai Hilltop. The turnoff to Indian Route 18 is about 30 miles west of Seligman on Route 66. Entry and camping permits are required.

69. Grand Canyon National Park

P.O. Box 129
Grand Canyon, AZ 86023
(928) 638-7888
www.nps.gov/grca

Location: Northern Arizona.
Description: Majestic canyon following 277 miles of the Colorado River.
How to get there: The South Rim is 80 miles north of Flagstaff. Take US 180
northwest to AZ 64 and go right (north) through Tusayan to the park's south
entrance. The North Rim is 44 miles south of Jacob Lake via AZ 67.

*I*n 1921, Alfred Bryan best described the Grand Canyon in words now
immortalized on postcards and posters: "I am 10,000 cathedrals rolled into
one." No matter what your faith, these miles of scenery will stir your soul.
You can never fully prepare for such an experience, whether you've gazed
upon the canyon once or see it every day.

Five million people visit the Grand Canyon annually, but the park is so
large that you can find quiet places just to sit at the edge and contemplate
the inner depths of your soul. The place overwhelms you so much that
looming problems vanish, leaving you refreshed and connected to something
greater than yourself.

Five tribes—the Hopi, Navajo, Havasupai, Paiute, and Hualapai—call
the canyon and its surrounding areas home, and places throughout the
canyon hold particular spiritual significance. The canyon hosts a diversity of
activities including Native American dances, New Age vision quests, and
the most inspiring Easter sunrise service on the planet.

Grand Canyon Community Church, (928) 638-2340, sponsors the
annual Easter sunrise service at the Grand Canyon's rim at Mather Point.
On the day that Christians around the world celebrate the resurrection of
Christ—their holiest day of the year—hundreds gather in the dark cold at
Mather Point, waiting for the first rays of sunshine to illuminate one of
God's masterpieces of creation.

The canyon's first Easter sunrise service was conducted near Bright
Angel Lodge in 1902. The Rev. Thomas C. Moffet, a Presbyterian minister,
made the two-day trip on horseback from Prescott to lead the service. An
account of that service written up in *The Coconino Sun* begins: "At Bright

Angel Trail, in the Grand Canyon, Easter morning dawned most gloriously. All nature bade God's people worship the Risen Lord." The story continues, "For some of us surely no dearer memory can linger with us."

The South Rim is open year-round, 24 hours a day. Visitor services and facilities inside the national park on the North Rim are open from mid-May to mid-October. For more information on ceremonies and events, please contact the Grand Canyon Chamber of Commerce at (928) 527-0359.

70. Sacred White Buffalo

Spirit Mountain Ranch
P.O. Box 31106
Flagstaff, AZ 86003
(928) 606-2779
E-mail: spirit@sacredwhitebuffalo.org
www.sacredwhitebuffalo.org

Jim and Dena Riley didn't set out to become the guardians of the sacred white buffalo that fulfill a Lakota Sioux prophecy. They simply liked the noble animals and bought one to graze the grass on their 66-acre South Dakota ranch.

With the birth of Miracle Moon, the first of four white buffalo they would own, everything changed. Miracle Moon, so named because she survived an accident right after her birth, came into the world red like all baby buffalo. Then her color began to change. At six months old, she was golden. At nine months old, she was white.

Though puzzled, the Rileys knew Miracle Moon was special. Although some people have tried to breed white cattle with buffalo to create a white buffalo, DNA testing confirmed that Miracle Moon was neither a mixed breed nor albino, but pure buffalo.

Location: About 20 miles north of Flagstaff.
Description: The home of the sacred white buffalo from the Lakota prophecy.
How to get there: From Flagstaff, take US 180 north. The ranch is on the right (east) side of the road past milepost 236.

Miracle Moon was born on April 30, 1997, the birthday of Arvol Looking Horse, the keeper of the pipe of the sacred White Buffalo Calf Woman from Lakota legend. The pipe is kept on the Cheyenne River Indian Reservation in South Dakota.

In the Lakota story, the Creator sent the White Buffalo Calf Woman to teach people how to pray with the pipe and to perform seven sacred ceremonies. The prophecy predicts that the White Buffalo Calf Woman will return in a time of chaos as a sign for all races to come together in peace and harmony. The appearance of the female white buffalo heralds a time of enlightenment and healing. Some believe that it signifies a spiritual shift and that prayers are being heard.

Jim and Dena Riley moved to their Arizona ranch in 2001. Since then, Native Americans have left a peace pole on the Rileys' property to show that the couple can be trusted. People have tied bundles of herbs or tobacco wrapped in vibrant, multihued fabric to the fence in honor of the buffalo and as prayers for their health and safety. With views of the San Francisco Peaks, Spirit Mountain Ranch faces a clearing of trees that is shaped like a buffalo. The form grows particularly evident when snow highlights this buffalo-shaped patch of ground surrounded by dark green trees—an uncanny allusion to the white buffalo, courtesy of Mother Nature.

Miracle Moon gave birth to Rainbow Spirit, Mandella Peace Pilgrim, and Arizona Spirit in 2000, 2001, and 2002, respectively. Rather than being bathed every day, the white buffalo hang out in the large corrals and loll about in the dirt with the rest of the herd. So instead of sporting snowy white coats, the buffalo wear earth tones of reddish-brown.

Eager to share the story of the buffalo, the Rileys plan to open a gift shop with information about the buffalo and a video screening of Miracle Moon's birth. Admission to the ranch is free but donations are graciously accepted.

71. San Francisco Peaks

Coconino National Forest
Peaks Ranger District
5075 N. Hwy. 89
Flagstaff, AZ 86004
(928) 526-0866
www.fs.fed.us/r3/coconino/

The San Francisco Peaks dominate northern Arizona's landscape. Native Americans revere these dark mountains set against bright blue skies. The peaks stir awe within everyone else. Views from their high vistas stretch for 80 miles, clear to the Grand Canyon's North Rim.

The peaks are home to the kachinas, the Hopi deities who fly to the Hopi villages each year, bringing rain with them. In Navajo belief, the range is the northernmost and the most sacred of the mountains that mark the four directions.

The mountains ring 12,643-foot Humphreys Peak, the highest point in Arizona. The elevation is so lofty that snow lingers here even as spring warms the towns below.

Contact the ranger station for information on the numerous picnic grounds, camping areas, and hiking trails in the area.

Location: North of Flagstaff.

Description: The most sacred mountain range revered by the Hopi, Navajo, and other area tribes.

How to get there: Many roads and trails cover the San Francisco Peaks. One hike is the Bear Jaw/Pipeline Road/Abineau Canyon Loop, a strenuous 7-mile loop that takes four or five hours; for an easier trip, just hike part of it. From Flagstaff, go north for 17 miles on US 89. Go left (west) on Forest Road 420 (across from the Sunset Crater turnoff). Go 0.2 mile and turn right (north) onto FR 552. Drive 1.3 miles to FR 418 and go right (north). Drive 7.6 miles (the road will head west) to FR 9123J. Go left (south) 0.7 mile to the trailhead.

72. Wupatki National Monument

Flagstaff Area National Monuments
6400 N. Hwy. 89
Flagstaff, AZ 86004
(928) 526-1157
E-mail: FLAG_Superintendent@nps.gov
www.nps.gov/wupa/

*O*n its 3,300 acres, Wupatki National Monument contains more than 2,000 pueblo sites, nearly 200 of them with seven to 10 rooms. These sites are connected ancestrally to the Hopi, Zuni, and Navajo, who call them sacred.

The largest one, the Wupatki Pueblo, is located behind the visitors' center. From there, the Wupatki Pueblo Trail leads you on an easy, 0.5-mile round-trip tour of the pueblo. The masonry pueblo was built gradually, beginning in the 1100s, and grew until it had 100 rooms and a ball court. The pueblo stood three stories high in some places and the first story had no exterior doors.

At the end of the Wupatki Pueblo Trail, inside an unobtrusive structure that looks like a square well, a breeze escapes from the ground through a blowhole. Even on a hot summer day, the blowhole emits a cool breeze that smells of damp earth. The people who lived here long ago might have attached spiritual significance to this air blowing from underground.

The other large pueblos on the site—Wukoki, Citadel, and Nalakihu— each have easy, short trails with paved roads leading up to them. You must stay on the trails to protect the fragile terrain and archaeological treasures. Backcountry hiking is prohibited.

Pay a visit to the overlook 200 feet from the visitors' center, from which you can view Sunset Crater, a volcano that erupted in A.D. 1065. Far away from the pueblo, black ash still covers the landscape.

The entry fee is $3 per person, with children 16 and under admitted free. The admission is good for seven days and includes access to Sunset Crater Volcano National Monument, as well.

Location: North of Flagstaff.
Description: Ancient pueblos and pit houses left behind by ancestors of the Hopi, Zuni, and Navajo.
How to get there: From Flagstaff, take US 89 north for 12 miles. Go right (east) at the sign for Sunset Crater Volcano/Wupatki National Monument (Forest Road 545) and continue 21 miles to the visitors' center. You'll pass the visitors' center for Sunset Crater Volcano National Monument, which also is worth a stop.

73. Spider Rock

Canyon de Chelly National Monument
P.O. Box 588
Chinle, AZ 86503
(928) 674-5500
E-mail: ailema_benally@nps.gov
www.nps.gov/cach/

According to Navajo belief, there are holy beings that inhabit Canyon de Chelly (pronounced da-SHAY). The spire of Spider Rock, a sacred place of Spider Woman, rises from the canyon bottom to an impressive height of 800 feet—just 245 feet shy of the Washington Monument.

The Navajo story tells that Spider Woman lived in a hole in the ground, but she liked to visit Spider Rock. From there, she helped the Twin Warriors find their Father Sun, who gave the warriors weapons to slay the monsters and save the people. Spider Woman also taught the Navajo how to weave.

Early basket-makers occupied the canyon from at least A.D. 350. Anasazi cliff dwellings dating from the 11th and 12th centuries also linger here. Members of the Navajo Tribe still live in the canyon today, and they leave offerings and say prayers at the base of Spider Rock.

Location: Near Chinle.

Description: An 800-foot-tall rock spire in a sacred canyon; the place where Spider Woman helped the Twin Warriors in Navajo belief.

How to get there: The visitors' center is 3 miles from US 191 in Chinle. Spider Rock Overlook is about 16 miles from the visitors' center at the end of South Rim Drive.

Canyon de Chelly has seen its share of violence and strife. In 1805, soldiers and Western settlers killed 115 Navajo people in Massacre Cave in Canyon del Muerte, the north fork of Canyon de Chelly. And during the Long Walk, the Navajo were forced out of Canyon de Chelly and their homeland to New Mexico. When treaties finally granted the Navajo access to their lands, thousands died on the march back. In 1868, the last peace treaty was signed and the first boundaries were drawn for the Navajo Reservation, with Canyon de Chelly at its center.

The visitors' center is open 8 a.m. to 5 p.m. daily from October through April, and 8 a.m. to 6 p.m. from May to September. It is closed on Christmas Day. Entrance for vehicles is free.

Overlooks line the 22-mile drive along the canyon's rim. You cannot enter the canyon without a Navajo guide and a National Park Service permit (unless you plan to hike the 2.5-mile White House Ruins Trail). Once you secure your guide and permit, you can hike or take your four-wheel-drive vehicle into the canyon. You can hire a guide at the visitors' center for about $15 an hour, with a three-hour minimum. Many visitors opt to go with a tour company for an hour or a day-long adventure; packages range in price from $45 per person to more than $125.

Region Five
Sedona and Vicinity

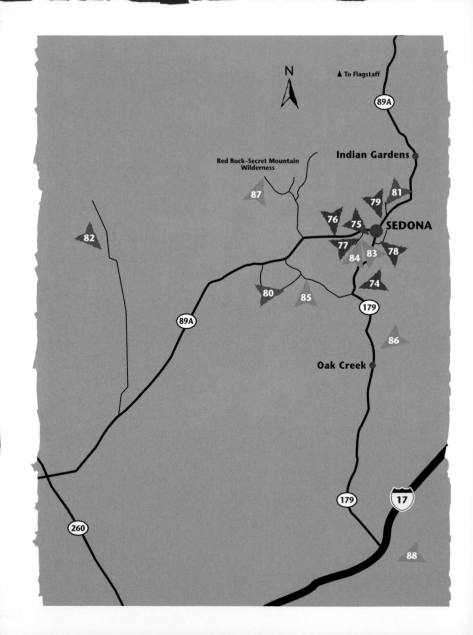

N

▲ To Flagstaff

89A

Red Rock–Secret Mountain Wilderness

Indian Gardens

87

81

79

82

76

75

SEDONA

77

78

84 83

74

80 85

179

89A

86

Oak Creek

179

17

260

88

"I wanted to change my life." That's what people say time and time again when asked what drew them to Sedona—a land of beautiful red rocks standing tall against a bright blue sky, a testament to God's beauty in nature.

Sedona, one man says, helps you find what you want in your life. Sedona, a woman says, is a gateway to a new consciousness. People come here looking for a spiritual awakening, for spiritual revelation. Some come to Sedona to participate in Native American vision quests. Others come to stay a week and never leave.

Just a decade ago, Sedona was a quieter place known for its scenic hiking and biking trails, as well as a movie-star haven and a backdrop for Westerns. Today, the town serves as a New Age center with many people and places that foster and teach the way of Spirit. Psychics, aura readers, and crystal shops commingle with a few crosses here and there.

According to a Northern Arizona University study, of the four million people who visit Sedona annually, at least 64 percent come seeking a spiritual experience. Traffic escalates on the weekends, yet silence prevails at the town's fringes.

The primary attractions are the major vortexes, or centers of the Earth's energy, that dot the landscape here. The rock formations that mark the sites of

several vortexes motivate and empower those who come near. The ancient peoples who left behind petroglyphs felt the energy of the place, as do modern visitors. Some people theorize that the iron oxide found in the formations, which lends the rocks their red color, draws the energy from the earth.

A Red Rock Pass, available almost everywhere in Sedona, grants you access to the vortex sites located on national forest land. A daily pass is $5 per vehicle, a weekly pass is $15, and an annual pass is $20. The fee goes toward maintaining the sites and educating the public about this alluring area.

These sacred sites, popular places for meditation, emit different kinds of earth energy, either calming or invigorating. Many people have reported having mystical experiences here.

Guide services in Sedona help you to experience the magic, and detailed maps assist you in locating the vortexes. When seeking out vortexes, guides suggest looking for the most twisted juniper trees because the branches spiral in response to the area's energy.

Enlightenment is not guaranteed, though. "Sometimes visitors will come back and say, 'We went out to that area, but there are no signs out there.' Well, there are no signs to the vortexes," says longtime Sedona resident Anita Dalton, founder of the Center for the New Age.

May you know it when you find it.

Earth Mother Father Foundation

Sanctuaries

74. Chapel of the Holy Cross

780 Chapel Rd.
Sedona, AZ 86336
(928) 282-4069

Sedona's most enduring religious symbol cannot be found in a crystal shop, but in the Chapel of the Holy Cross. The chapel was the dream of local resident and sculptor Marguerite Brunswig Staude, who hoped it would function as "a spiritual fortress so charged with God, that it spurs man's spirit godward."

Chapel of the Holy Cross appears to grow out of the red rocks that support it. A large cross that spans the structure's height and width dominates the facade, and windows surround the cross. The base of the cross lodges between the rocks on the 250-foot-high pinnacled spur.

From within the simple chapel, the cross frames views of the mountains. Although the parking lot seems perpetually full of cars, you

Location: South of Sedona.

Description: A chapel emblematic of Sedona and open to all.

How to get there: From downtown Sedona, go 3 miles south on AZ 179, then left (east) on Chapel Road. The chapel is at the end of road.

always can find time for quiet prayer and meditation without interruption. Once chatty visitors step inside, a hush falls over them as they light candles for the intentions of their prayers.

Marguerite Brunswig Staude first envisioned such a monument to God when observing the Empire State Building's construction in 1932. She wrote, "When viewed from a certain angle, a cross seemed to impose itself through the very core of the structure." Her dream came true with the Chapel of the Holy Cross, a place where "the church may come to life in the souls of men and be a living reality."

The chapel was completed in 1956 and dedicated to the memory of Staude's parents in 1957. Chapel of the Holy Cross is part of the Roman Catholic Diocese of Phoenix, but has not been an active parish since the 1960s. Staude was Roman Catholic, but the chapel welcomes all. New Age practitioners say that the chapel is situated on a vortex and emits sacred energy from the earth.

The chapel and its gift shop are open from 9 a.m. to 5 p.m. Monday through Saturday, and 10 a.m. to 5 p.m. on Sunday. A prayer service commences at 5 p.m. on Monday. The chapel closes on Thanksgiving, Christmas, Good Friday, and Easter. The chapel and gift shop have no public facilities. Admission is free.

For those who would like to attend regular Roman Catholic Mass in Sedona, visit St. John Vianney Catholic Church at 180 Soldiers Pass Road. The church holds a daily Mass at 8 a.m., a Vigil Mass at 5:30 p.m. on Saturday, and Sunday Mass at 8 a.m. and 10:30 a.m. A Spanish Mass takes place at 6 p.m. on Sunday. For more information on St. John Vianney's services, call (928) 282-7545.

75. Center for the New Age

341 Hwy. 179
Sedona, AZ 86336
(928) 282-2085
www.sedonanewagecenter.com

*T*he rushing sound of Oak Creek soothes as you sit on the yoga platform outside the Center for the New Age. Inside, you'll find the largest New Age bookstore in Sedona, along with more than 20 psychics, healers, and teachers to help you find enlightenment and your spiritual path.

Spirit led Anita Dalton to this multi-acre property with wonderful energy. "Spirit woke me up in the middle of the night and said, 'Do this,'" she recalls. "I had no idea what it was going to look like." Dalton—the center's founder and one of the first New Age practitioners to open for business in Sedona—says that centuries ago, ancient people used the site as ceremonial ground.

Location: Southeast Sedona.

Description: A center that brings together retreats, workshops, psychics, and healers, along with a bookstore and crystal shop.

How to get there: The center is where AZ 179 and AZ 89A meet, across the street from Tlaquepaque, a retail center with restaurants.

Center for the New Age runs retreats but has no on-site lodging. Opportunities include aura readings, chakra cleansings, Native American drumming circles, and a sweat lodge. It distributes free vortex maps, which staff members—including Dalton's daughter and center co-owner Jamie Butler, the author of *Sedona's Best Vortex Guidebook*—can explain in detail.

An aura photograph and reading cost about $30. The machine takes a picture of you with your energy field superimposed in bursts of color around your head. To read your energy, you place your hands on sensors that register electromagnetic fields. You can get a sense of your spirituality and learn what adjustments to make in your life for optimum joy. A prevalence of pink, for example, means you are sensitive, emotional, and feminine. Yellow shows that you are intellectual with a talent for organization and discipline. Magenta indicates spiritual perceptiveness.

As you wander the grounds, you can stop for a moment at the foot of the energy-focusing copper pyramids. The building's exterior displays a colorful mural painted in 1996 by Christopher Scott titled "Creative." It depicts people of all ages and races holding hands around the earth in a symbol of peace and harmony.

Center for the New Age maintains a sense of humor and is not above making a little joke about Sedona's New Age reputation: At the bookstore, you can buy Sedona Vortex-in-a-Can with a "lifetime(s) guarantee." But the real guarantee is that at Center for the New Age, you'll discover many new paths to higher consciousness.

76. Earth Mother Father Foundation

2144 W. Hwy. 89A
Sedona, AZ 86336
(928) 204-1933
E-mail: emff@emff.org
www.emff.org

Spirit inspires much in Sedona. At the Earth Mother Father Foundation, founder Mary-Margareht Rose has built a place to honor her vision of healing the Earth and humanity "by moving each forward on their unique path with greater courage, balance, dignity, gratefulness, and understanding."

You can enhance your healing and intuitive abilities in these calm surroundings on 10 acres. Rose, a healer, worked with Native American grandmothers to design the gardens. The property has a medicine wheel, a vortex, a Mother Mary Meditation Area, and a Lord Sananda Meditation Area.

The traditional Lakota Sioux medicine wheel is a place to heal and pray, and the crystals and stones that lace its circular path enhance its power. When you walk the medicine wheel, always clockwise, you ask God or Spirit permission to enter. You can feel the yes or no answer.

The most noticeable structure here is the Great Pyramid of Sedona, built by Thomas Hunt, who says he channeled angels to guide him in its design. Inside the multicolored pyramid, he conducts attunements in the sound chamber, a practice with both health and spiritual benefits.

Location: West Sedona.

Description: A New Age center to help you walk your path and nurture spiritual growth.

How to get there: The center is on AZ 89A, just west of Coffee Pot Drive and across from the Harkins Theatres.

Hunt spent three years building the copper, aluminum, and steel structure. He drew from all religions and from the inspiration of the angels who taught him the suppressed story of creation. According to Hunt, Adam and Eve were two angelic beings who came to Earth in innocence. Eve allowed herself to be worshiped and Adam felt separated. They fell into the realms of the emotions, marking the beginning of the spiritual transformation of the planet. Different religions developed as part of humanity's attempt to understand this occurrence.

The pyramid's interior walls illustrate 600,000 years of history. The symbols on the walls honor the 288 names of God in Hebrew and Sanskrit. Geometry blends with drawings of Jesus.

Once a month, the pyramid is open for public meditation at no charge. The pyramid healing program is six days long and costs about $3,500.

The foundation also has a 3,800-pound Brazilian crystal embedded with black tourmaline. Crystals magnify the energies of the vortex and of Sedona.

Those at Earth Mother Father Foundation give credit to the Creator for all they do and for allowing their energies to blend. Rose uses the Nolatarean Approach, a healing technique channeled from beings that live on an undiscovered planet in this solar system. They are human and honor the same God-presence, but they are more advanced, she says.

The center is open from 10 a.m. to 6 p.m. daily. A meditation is held at noon daily; each night at 7:30, a different metaphysical program takes place. Starlight Community Church meets here on Friday nights.

On Sundays at 10:30 a.m. Mountain time, the center broadcasts "The Gathering" online at www.emff.org. The online spiritual gathering combines music, meditation, group healing, and a central message.

77. Rainbow Ray Focus

225 Airport Rd.
Sedona, AZ 86336
(928) 282-3427

*R*ainbow Ray Focus teaches a way of life through Jesus Christ Ananda. "Ananda" is the highest name given to Christ. It's not in the Bible, but is a belief taught by New Agers, says the Rev. Rosemarie Witte, the spiritual leader here.

Founded in 1965, the congregation works with masters of light from other planes of existence. Sunday services are at 11 a.m., with another meeting on Thursday nights. The informal meetings are without ritual. Those who gather here sing and pray, meditate and heal. Witte usually performs a channeling at the end, but she allows anyone to share intuitive and spiritual abilities. "We go with the flow and let the Spirit bring in the beauty of what we can share with one another, and there's lots of love," she describes. Congregants believe that Christ died on the cross and made his ascension so that we may have full consciousness.

The chapel is small and simple, and the attached patio opens to fabulous Sedona mountain views. Rainbow Ray Focus is located just below the Airport Mesa Vortex, and you can feel the energy nearby. The peaceful grounds have a garden open for meditation, with permission. Everyone is invited to attend services and meetings.

Location: West Sedona, near the airport.
Description: A New Age congregation honoring Jesus Christ Ananda.
How to get there: From AZ 89A, go south on Airport Road. The driveway into Rainbow Ray Focus, marked by a small sign, will be on your right.

78. Sedona Creative Life Center

333 Schnebly Hill Rd.
Sedona, AZ 85336
(928) 282-9300
E-mail: info@sedonacreativelife.com
www.sedonacreativelife.com

*B*uilt using ecologically sound principles to minimize negative impact on the environment, the Sedona Creative Life Center merges harmoniously with the land. Only the point of the glass-covered chapel reaches out above the trees and to the sky.

With a wide array of programs for people of all ages and beliefs, the nonprofit center is a place for spiritual and creative growth. The center provides tools to enlighten the mind, body, and spirit through seminars, creative workshops, speakers of local and national renown, concerts and theater, art programs, and children's workshops.

Sedona Creative Life Center was founded to celebrate the human spirit and provide an uplifting and nourishing environment for the heart and soul. The proprietors don't expect everyone to embrace all that they offer, only to honor it, as you would honor life.

Location: Southeast Sedona.
Description: A spiritual and creative growth conference center for large and small groups set in beautiful surroundings.
How to get there: From AZ 179, go east on Schnebly Hill Road. The center will be on your left.

Some of the featured speakers and performers at Sedona Creative Life Center have included Ram Dass, Don Miguel Ruiz, Dr. David R. Hawkins, and numerous concerts with artists such as Will Ackerman, William Eaton, and Chris Spheeris.

The monthly "Poetry at the Center" series spotlights national award-winning poets. The center also hosts grant-writing workshops, cooking retreats, a summer children's art camp, a monthly full-moon meditation and lecture, and annual seminars with Gita Saraydarian on Ageless Wisdom and the teachings of her father, Torkom Saraydarian.

On 15 acres just minutes from downtown, the center has space to accommodate programs with up to 225 attendees; other rooms seat from 20 to 100. If catering is requested for certain programs, the center will provide you with names of approved services and will assist with some forms of event promotion. The types of programs at the Sedona Creative Life Center should mesh with the center's philosophy, "a spiritual world view characterized by global concern, social conscience, peaceful coexistence, and ecological sustainability," according to its mission statement.

The center offers its beautiful glass-steepled chapel for weddings. The intimate setting seats up to 50 people. Outside are a circular patio, a flagged trail, beautiful sculpture gardens, and secluded nooks ideal for meditation. Gardens for Humanity—a nonprofit organization that builds sustainable, healing gardens—is also working on developing a "Peace Garden" that will be used by the Karmapa, a Tibetan spiritual leader, to give teachings and blessings.

79. Wayside Chapel, Community Church of Sedona

401 N. Hwy. 89A
Sedona, AZ 86336
(928) 282-4262

Mailing address:
P.O. Box M
Sedona, AZ 86339

*W*ayside Chapel brought the glory of God in word and song to Sedona's red rocks, which long had reflected the majesty of God in silence. Traveling preacher Albert C. Stewart of the American Sunday School Union came to Sedona in 1918. The union wanted to establish Sunday school classes throughout the West to teach the essential truths held in common by evangelical denominations, as well as to found congregations to eventually build churches.

For 30 years, the classes met in a small schoolhouse, which burned down because of a lightning strike. In 1947, the current land was donated for a nondenominational chapel. Town namesake Sedona Schnebly, the wife of the postmaster, acted as secretary-treasurer for the group that raised money for the first church building and its bell. A second story

Location: Uptown Sedona.
Description: An evangelical Christian church that began as a Sunday school class more than 80 years ago.
How to get there: From AZ 179 heading north, go right (north) on AZ 89A. The church is on the left side of the road, past the offices, restaurants, and shops.

was added to the structure in 1974 to meet the needs of the growing congregation. The church's first organ is on display at the Sedona Heritage Museum.

In the church's early days, a time when travel and life were difficult in the West, its members contemplated the goodness of God in providing such a place of worship. Moses' request, "I beseech thee, O Lord, show me thy Glory," served as a guiding principle, as did the Lord's reply, "I will put thee in the cleft of the rock and will cover thee there with my hand."

The nondenominational church helps its members grow in Christ and spread the word of Jesus through worldwide missions. It teaches that the Bible is the inspired, infallible, and unchanging word of God, and that it is the only rule, entirely sufficient for Christian living and faith. The congregation also believes that the grace of God, Christ's completed work on the cross, and faith in Christ alone are the only paths to salvation.

Community Church of Sedona's pastor, the Rev. Paul Wallace, hails from a fifth-generation Sedona family. Sunday Bible study commences at 9:15 a.m. and worship takes place at 10:30 a.m. Parking is available behind the church.

Retreats

80. Cathedral Rock Lodge and Retreat Center

61 W. Los Amigos Lane
Sedona, AZ 86336
(928) 282-7608
E-mail: info@cathedralrocklodge.com
www.cathedralrocklodge.com

*T*he Cathedral Rock Lodge and Retreat Center is more than a scenic spot to stay while visiting Sedona. It's a place of spiritual renewal and healing connected with the Aquarian Concepts Community, a group of people who work together, live together, and support each other in a community based on shared spiritual values.

The three charming retreat houses have telephones, televisions, and VCRs. The largest of the three starts at $160 a night for two people, and the smallest one costs about $110 a night for two people. Additional guests are $20 extra; children are welcome. The cottages, complete with kitchens, rival pleasant bed-and-breakfast accommodations.

This is one of several enterprises of the Aquarian Concepts Community, started in 1989 by Gabriel of Sedona and Niánn Emerson Chase. About 100 "fully aligned" people live in the community. They follow the teachings of Gabriel and The Urantia Book—a book they believe was authored by celestial beings as a special revelation to this planet—published in 1995 by the Urantia Foundation. Its teachings include that all humans are the sons and daughters of one God, the Universal Father.

Location: West Sedona.

Description: A retreat and renewal center affiliated with the Aquarian Concepts Community and Gabriel of Sedona.

How to get there: From AZ 89A, go south on Upper Red Rock Loop (which turns into Red Rock Loop) for about 3 miles. Cathedral Rock Lodge and Retreat Center will be on your left, where West Los Amigos Lane connects with Red Rock Loop.

Gabriel was drawn to Sedona as the planetary sacred home for the community he would cofound. According to community members, the area was a site sacred to Native Americans who met there to talk to ancestors who had passed away to the other side.

Within walking distance of Cathedral Rock Lodge and Retreat Center, Avalon Gardens extends 16 acres along Oak Creek. Visitors may make appointments to view the gorgeous gardens, which feature raised beds of flowers and organic vegetables. Guests of the retreat center are admitted free of charge, but other visitors must pay an admission fee.

Most Sundays at 10:30 a.m., a spiritual service is held on the grounds at the main amphitheater. Built into the red rocks near a wide and deep part of Oak Creek, a smaller amphitheater is home to the Wheel of Revelation, an adaptation of a Native American medicine wheel made of stones and cornmeal. The divine patterns of nature, the four seasons and the four directions, connect to relationships and life.

Under the community's umbrella, members also run Spirit Steps Tours, which provides vortex and other mystical experiences. Its Cosmic Wheel of Destiny ceremony, according to www.spiritsteps.org, "blends traditional spiritual teachings with present-day divine revelation, inspiring us to live in harmony and cooperation with natural and celestial forces resident on our planet." The community also maintains a recording studio called Future Studios, where they make "Global Change Music," as well as a home study program and a school.

The members view themselves as part of a spiritual renaissance and desire to effect unity in the new millennium. The community wants to manifest the fruits of God's spirit and bring justice and actualization to all the people of the planet. Through this path, these sons and daughters of God are on their way to becoming like God the father and God the mother. If you really want to reach out to God, God can reach back, members say.

For more information about Aquarian Concepts, stop by the office at 2940 Southwest Drive in Sedona, call (928) 204-1206, or visit the website at www.aquarianconcepts.org.

81. The Healing Center of Arizona

25 Wilson Canyon Rd.
Sedona, AZ 86336
(928) 282-7710
www.sedonahealingcenter.com

The Healing Center of Arizona invites people of all faiths to convene under its geodesic domes. John Paul Weber founded the center in 1979, long before Sedona became inundated with tourists and places for spiritual growth. Weber took seven years to build the center by hand, using mostly recycled materials. The white exterior stands out from the red rocks and green trees. Inside, the white walls and carpet create a serene ambience.

The retreat center has four rooms, each painted with different murals. Big groups can sleep in the larger domed space, and the center boasts one of the few geodesic dome tree houses in existence.

Healing work takes place in the meditation dome's amplifying chamber, which enhances curative qualities. Even if you lightly brush your bare toes across the carpet, the sound resonates loudly throughout the room.

For various effects, you can place different crystals atop and then sit inside the chakra-cleansing pyramid built by a man in Sedona. The pyramid focuses energy downward to clear blocked chakras, the points inside your body that allow energy to flow through.

Weber has lived in Sedona for more than 44 years. He spent 16 years in San Francisco teaching college courses on meditation, yoga, Native American shamanism, biofeedback, altered states of consciousness, Tibetan healing arts, and other mind-body-spirit subjects. A nurse with a psychology degree, he cofounded The Healing Center in San Francisco in 1976 as a place to foster healing without drugs or surgery. He always found himself drawn back to Sedona and finally returned to start The Healing Center of Arizona.

The center follows the teachings of Krishna, Buddha, Jesus, White Eagle, and Sri Aurobindo, but

Location: North Sedona.

Description: A place devoted to holistic health practices and integration of the body, emotion, mind, and spirit.

How to get there: From AZ 89A, go north on Jordan Road. Turn right (east) on Hillside Avenue, then take an immediate left (north) on Mountain View Drive. Turn right (east) on Wilson Canyon Road.

honors all religions. It hosts concerts and sweat lodges, and also offers numerous therapies from health and nutritional counseling to past-life regression.

The center grows an organic vegetable garden and is building a seed bank. In the garden, the 52 rose bushes arc in the shape of a rainbow. A medicine wheel is made out of crystals, and a plaque remembers past healers of Sedona. For recreation, a trampoline awaits across the street, as do a swimming hole and rope swing at nearby Oak Creek.

The center offers group and personalized retreats. The guest rooms start at around $70, while a sleepover in the large dome costs less per person. Individual rooms are private with a shared bath, and the accommodations equal those of finer hotels. Guests may prepare their own meals or, with advance reservations, dine on gourmet vegetarian dishes.

82. Sedona Mago Garden

3500 E. Bill Gray Rd.
Sedona, AZ 86336
(928) 282-4300
E-mail: sedonamagogarden@hotmail.com
www.sedonamagogarden.org

A group of Koreans and Americans brings ancient wisdom from the Far East to this retreat center, the 149-acre Sedona Mago Garden. "Mago" is Korean for Mother Earth. The healing and philosophy of the Sedona Mago Garden incorporate Taoist philosophy through the practice of Dahnhak—"dahn" meaning energy and "hak" meaning study. This natural healing system restores balance and helps you attain spiritual awakening by harnessing "ki," a universal energy. Through this 2,000-year-old Korean practice, exercise and meditation lead to spiritual growth.

Location: West of Sedona.

Description: A place of solitude for the Korean spiritual practice of Dahnhak.

How to get there: From Sedona, go southwest on AZ 89A and turn right (west) on Bill Gray Road, which is 200 feet north of milepost 358. Continue almost 11 miles on Bill Gray Road, a dirt road usually suitable for sedans, and turn left on Sedona Retreat Road to the facility's entrance.

The adobe-style buildings seemingly disappear into the red rocks surrounding the property. A student of Frank Lloyd Wright designed the complex. As a contrast, white teepees jump out of the landscape; the teepees make for a fun, though more rustic, place to spend the night.

The resort-style guest rooms and casitas each have private bathrooms, and the facility accommodates up to 100 guests. Only vegetarian meals appear on the menu, in keeping with the pure environment. Rooms range from $90 to $120 per night. The fee includes three meals, but programs cost extra.

Programs of various lengths include fasting, meridian exercises, and energy practice at vortexes on the property and in Sedona. The one- to three-week Intensive Dahn Discovery helps you develop your personal power centers for better health, more energy, and peace of mind.

The 12 vortexes here allow you to embark upon a "meditative journey to the inner self and meet the soul of the Earth," according to the center's website. Opening the body's meridian points, or energy pathways, leads to invigoration and the improved functions of your major organs.

The mission of the center is to heal the body, the mind, humanity, and the Earth. The practice of Dahnhak is based on the belief in the original perfection of humanity, and its goal is to recover one's original perfection in the mind, body, and soul. The next step is to benefit the rest of the world by helping others to discover the same. Dr. Seung Heun Lee, who has written extensively on the subject and is a grand master and founder of the modern Dahnhak and Brain Respiration movements, sees this practice as a way to go from seeking enlightenment to acting it, from meditation to healing.

Sacred Places

83. Shrine of the Red Rocks

3 Shrine Rd.
Sedona, AZ 86336
(928) 282-9012

*A*bove Airport Mesa, a 25-foot-tall cross stands watch over the city, a counterpoint to the crystals and chakra cleansings prevalent here. The Eastern Star chapter at the Red Rock Memorial Lodge #63 put up the cross in 1961. Arizona Sen. Barry Goldwater dedicated the monument to the Masonic Lodge and to the people of Sedona.

On the concrete platform, a plaque says, "The Lord is risen indeed. Peace be unto you." Benches under the trees make for inviting places to sit.

The cross is lighted most nights, and in the dark skies of Sedona, the cross glows, almost appearing to hover over the mountains that disappear in the darkness. On particularly clear nights, you can see the cross from quite a distance.

The lodge's hall is available for rental. Religious services and weddings have taken place on the outdoor stage at Shrine of the Red Rocks.

Location: West Sedona, near the airport.
Description: A cross atop a mountain.
How to get there: From AZ 89A, go south on Airport Road. Take the left before the airport and follow the signs to the cross.

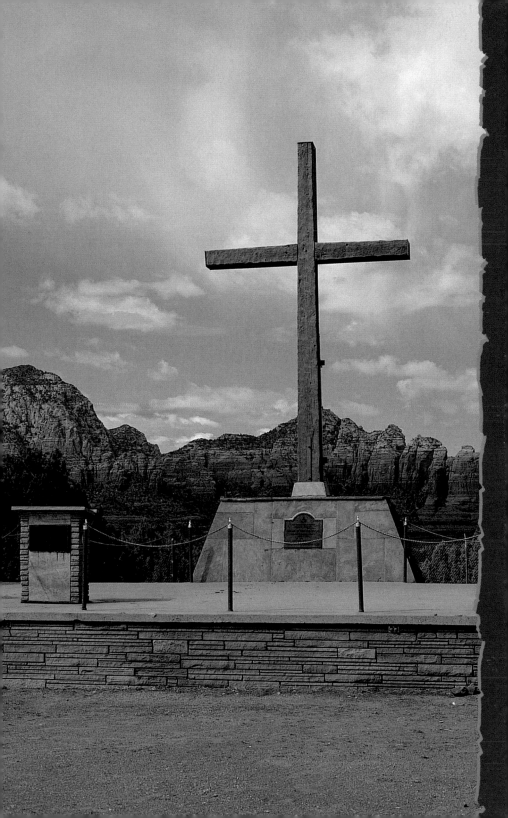

84. Airport Mesa Vortex

Coconino National Forest
Red Rock Ranger District
250 Brewer Rd.
Sedona, AZ 86336
(928) 282-4119
www.redrockcountry.org

Mailing address:
P.O. Box 300
Sedona, AZ 86339

*E*ach vortex bears different energy attributes. At Airport Mesa, the "masculine" energy is said to strengthen your decisiveness, self-confidence, and concentration.

The Rev. Rosemarie Witte, spiritual leader of the nearby Rainbow Ray Focus, says the energy gives her a feeling of warmth and elation. Some people describe tingles. People feel the flow of energy differently, depending on how they tune in.

Parking is close to the hiking trail, which is a steep but relatively easy walk to the vortex and the top of Airport Mesa. You don't need to go far, though, to experience the effects.

Jamie Butler, author of *Sedona's Best Vortex Guidebook*, suggests carrying an amethyst crystal in your pocket to increase the energy and enhance your spiritual and intuitive abilities. If the energy doesn't affect you, the gorgeous sunrises and sunsets with panoramic views of Sedona surely will.

Airport Mesa gets crowded, so plan to visit at dawn. A Red Rock Pass is required to park here. See the introduction to this region on pages 189–190 for information.

Location: West Sedona, near the airport.

Description: One of the major vortexes, or earth energy centers, in Sedona.

How to get there: From AZ 89A, go south on Airport Road to the parking area and trailhead, about 0.5 mile.

85. Cathedral Rock

Coconino National Forest
Red Rock Ranger District
250 Brewer Rd.
Sedona, AZ 86336
(928) 282-4119
www.redrockcountry.org

Mailing address:
P.O. Box 300
Sedona, AZ 86339

The tall spires of Cathedral Rock gave this formation its name. The red rocks reach skyward in two delicately thin and two wide formations.

This vortex strengthens the feminine side and enhances qualities such as compassion, kindness, and patience. It's a superb spot for a healing meditation to alleviate stress and pain. The energy is supposed to be strongest at the base of Cathedral Rock where Oak Creek flows closest by.

The entry fee into the recreation area is $5, and a Red Rock Pass is not required. The area also serves as a popular destination for those who enjoy picnicking and swimming.

Location: Red Rock Crossing–Crescent Moon Recreation Area, in southwest Sedona.
Description: One of the major vortexes, or earth energy centers, in Sedona.
How to get there: From AZ 89A, go south on Upper Red Rock Loop. Go almost 2 miles, turn left on Chavez Ranch Road, and continue 0.8 mile to the recreation area's entrance.

86. Bell Rock

Coconino National Forest
Red Rock Ranger District
250 Brewer Rd.
Sedona, AZ 86336
(928) 282-4119
www.redrockcountry.org

Mailing address:
P.O. Box 300
Sedona, AZ 86339

*B*ell Rock's shape distinguishes it from the numerous mountains surrounding Sedona. It's home to a vortex that strengthens all qualities: masculine, feminine, and balance. The feelings here have been called electric, intense, and motivating.

Achieving balance between the masculine and feminine selves holds importance because if you have too much feminine energy, others can easily take advantage of you. If you harbor too much masculine energy, you might take advantage of others and harm them. In the balance, you treat others the way you want them to treat you, with a blend of strength and compassion.

The paths are not difficult to hike, but be prepared. The life-force energy is so intense that people have felt it without walking very far. Only experienced hikers and climbers should try to ascend Bell Rock.

Parking spots exist along the road, and you will need a Red Rock Pass to park in them. See the introduction to this region on pages 189–190 for information.

Location: Between Sedona and the village of Oak Creek.

Description: One of the major vortexes, or earth energy centers, in the Sedona area.

How to get there: At milepost 307.5 on AZ 179, just north of the village of Oak Creek, is the south trailhead to Bell Rock. Park in the pullouts on the side of the road. It's an easy, 3.7-mile hike (one way) to the base of Bell Rock.

87. Boynton Canyon and the Red Rock–Secret Mountain Wilderness

Coconino National Forest
Red Rock Ranger District
250 Brewer Rd.
Sedona, AZ 86336
(928) 282-4119
www.redrockcountry.org

Mailing address:
P.O. Box 300
Sedona, AZ 86339

*B*oynton Canyon Trail leads to one of the Sedona area's main vortexes—a place that increases balance—but the canyon and its other hiking trails also are dotted with energy centers, pictographs, petroglyphs, and Native American ruins. The Boynton Canyon Trail, a moderate-level hiking trail, is 2.4 miles (one way) with an elevation change of 600 feet. When hiking in this area, stay on the trail and take plenty of water.

Location: Northwest of Sedona.

Description: A canyon with many hiking trails, Native American ruins, and vortex sites (earth energy centers).

How to get there: From AZ 89A, go north on Dry Creek Road (Forest Road 152C) for almost 3 miles. Go left (west) on Boynton Pass Road and continue 1.7 miles, then go right into a parking area. Signs point the way. From Trail No. 47, take the right fork (Vista Trail) to the main vortex site, a knoll with twisted juniper trees.

Other nearby trails and forest roads take you into the backcountry of Red Rock–Secret Mountain Wilderness. Native American ruins, petroglyphs, and smaller vortex sites distinguish the area.

The Honanki and Palatki pueblos, constructed by the Sinagua, also are cached in the Red Rock–Secret Mountain Wilderness. Instead of turning right into the trailhead parking area, continue on Boynton Pass Road, following the signs to FR 525. The Honanki site is about 5 miles north on FR 525. To access the Palatki site, go north on FR 525 for about 1 mile to FR 795 (a dirt road). Turn right (northwest) and continue about 1.5 miles to the site.

The sites share a visitors' center (928-282-4119) that explains the dwellings, built between 1130 and 1300. Remember to never touch or remove anything from archaeological sites.

Some of the dirt roads can be rough, especially after a rain, and they are only suitable for four-wheel-drive vehicles. Rather than risking the backcountry travel, you might choose to sign up for a Jeep tour. Find out about these tours—many of which include a spiritual component—at area visitors' centers and other places offering tourist information. Tours typically start at about $50 per person.

You will need a Red Rock Pass to visit any of these sites. See the introduction to this region on pages 189–190 for details.

88. V Bar V Ranch Heritage Site

Coconino National Forest
Red Rock Ranger District
250 Brewer Rd.
Sedona, AZ 86336
(928) 282-4119
www.redrockcountry.org

Mailing address:
P.O. Box 300
Sedona, AZ 86339

*I*n the cottonwood riparian forest along Wet Beaver Creek, more than 1,000 petroglyphs gather on one large sandstone panel, Arizona's most concentrated petroglyph site. For years, a working ranch sheltered the site from outsiders and preserved it in fine condition. After the ranch closed, the V Bar V Ranch Heritage Site opened to the public. A locked fence now protects the site after operating hours.

Location: South of Sedona.

Description: The most concentrated panel of petroglyphs in the state.

How to get there: From I-17, go southeast on Forest Road 618 (Exit 298, the junction where AZ 179 heads north to Sedona) for 2.5 miles. Go right at the sign that leads into the parking lot. Signs mark the way. The paved road turns into an easy dirt road.

The Sinaguans carved these petroglyphs between A.D. 650 and 1400. One symbol spirals and then goes off like a road; it might very well be the map to Montezuma Well, a sacred site connected with a Native American creation story and also a plentiful source of water. The panel might have served as an ancient message board. Animal symbols might signify hunting magic, and the male and female symbols might be associated with fertility.

Although you'll likely be hard-pressed to find solitude here, the site is well worth visiting. The concentration of petroglyphs in one place, rather than scattered throughout a larger area, overwhelms the senses.

The site is open 9:30 a.m. to 3:30 p.m. Friday through Monday, and the hike—less than 1 mile roundtrip—is easy enough for small children to handle. The ground is mostly flat and shaded by tall trees. A knowledgeable guide leads groups to the site, gives a brief lecture, and answers questions. The site also has a visitors' center, where you should meet the guide.

You will need a Red Rock Pass to visit this site. See the introduction to this region on pages 189–190 for information.

Region Six
East-Central Arizona

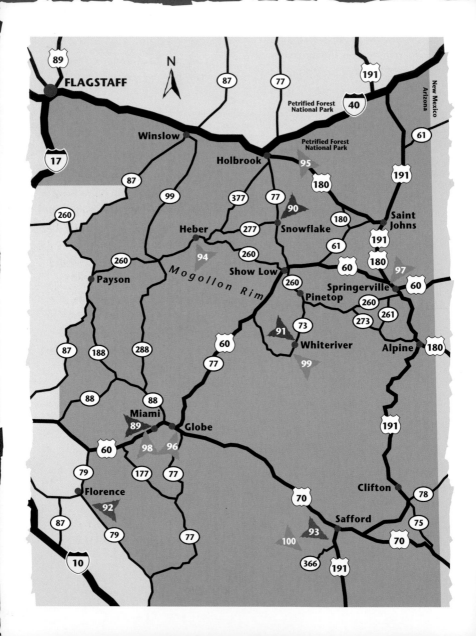

$\mathcal{T}$he unexpected and the historic define the sanctuaries, retreats, and sacred places of east-central Arizona, where summer temperatures are comfortable and the winters often bring snow. For example, the Church of the Open Bible Lutheran Apache Mission has served Whiteriver for almost a century. In this white clapboard building on the Fort Apache Indian Reservation, Chief Alchesay, the next to the last chief of the Apache, was baptized into the Christian faith. But today's White Mountain Apache Tribe also fosters traditional beliefs; visitors can learn more about such practices at its culture museum.

Snowflake is the proud home of the state's newest Mormon temple. When the temple opened for public tours, almost 93,000 people came to view the new facility —an impressive turnout, as Snowflake's population is only about 5,000.

At St. Anthony's Monastery, the Greek Orthodox Church has established a fascinating community in the desert. It's an elaborate property of beautiful churches, chapels, and retreat houses populated by monks who lead lives of prayer and work.

Within the Apache-Sitgreaves National Forest is Mt. Baldy, a site sacred to the Apache. The Mogollon Rim is home to places sacred not only to Native Americans but to people in the Wiccan and broader pagan community.

Crosses mark memorials along roadways throughout the state as remembrances of those who died in traffic accidents. On US 60 just south of Miami stands a roadside shrine more elaborate than most, a place to stop, pray, and light a candle for those so tragically lost.

Small towns pepper the region, some more out of the way than others. Most destinations are a five- to six-hour drive from metropolitan Phoenix. For city dwellers, the pace slows when away from rush-hour traffic and 24-hour grocery stores. The area's isolation only adds to the peace of these places, making them more than worth the drive.

Sanctuaries

89. Our Lady of the Blessed Sacrament

914 Sullivan St.
Miami, AZ 85539
(928) 473-3568

Mailing address:
P.O. Drawer E
Miami, AZ 85539

*E*very day, hundreds and hundreds of cars pass by this historic Catholic church just off US 60 in Miami. But when passersby duck off the highway and drop in for a visit, they find a blend of old and new, a place to stop and pray undisturbed.

Our Lady of the Blessed Sacrament was established in 1915 in the mining town of Miami as a parish to serve both Spanish- and English-speaking Catholics. The church still holds Mass in both languages.

Inside, beautiful and unique stained-glass windows surround the simple wooden pews. The parish added the windows about two years ago through a program in which parishioners donated money for each window and then chose the design. Some opted for windows that depict saints, but one window bears a lovely image of Mother Teresa.

Outside, a fountain bubbles at the feet of a statue of Jesus. The water flows over rocks that proclaim "peace" and "hope." The mature trees shade the courtyard and the nearby benches create an inviting space.

The church doors often are unlocked, so you can go inside and pray during office hours, 9 a.m. to 4:30 p.m. weekdays. If the doors are locked, go through the office. Weekend Masses take place at 6 p.m. Saturday and 8 a.m. and 10 a.m. Sunday. The 8 a.m. Mass is in Spanish.

Location: Miami.
Description: A historic Catholic church established to serve a bilingual parish.
How to get there: From US 60, go north on Reppy Avenue and right (east) on Sullivan Street. From US 60, you can see the church in the middle of Miami.

90. Snowflake Temple

1875 W. Canyon Dr.
Snowflake, AZ 85937
(928) 536-6626

*W*ith 11 million members across the globe, the Church of Jesus Christ of Latter-day Saints is the fifth largest denomination in the world. Yet, its teachings remain a mystery to many people. Central to that mystery is the temple, where sacred rites bind families and marriages together for all time.

Although only church members in good standing with a recommend from a bishop may enter a Mormon temple after its dedication ceremony, the public can tour it beforehand. In February 2002, Arizonans had their first chance to view the interior of a temple since the renovation of Mesa's temple in 1975. People came from far and wide: Nearly 93,000 people viewed the temple during two weeks, and Snowflake has just 5,000 residents.

Snowflake's temple is the second one in the state and the 108th in the world. When Mormon pioneers began settling the area in the late 1870s, church leaders planned to build the state's first temple in Snowflake. As Arizona's population grew, church membership swelled in Mesa and Phoenix, so the temple was built there instead.

In Snowflake, the 17,500-square-foot temple made of both royal peach and rose granite now crowns the piñon-covered butte where Boy Scouts once camped. The church's president and prophet, Gordon S. Hinckley, dedicated the temple on March 3, 2002.

Outside the temple, water cascades over ledges of natural rock and into a pool. A golden statue of the angel Moroni perches atop the temple's spire, facing east. The ancient prophet and a central figure in the Book of Mormon symbolizes preaching the restored gospel of Jesus Christ to the world.

The territorial Victorian style of the Snowflake Temple reflects its surroundings, bearing influences from the area's Mormon pioneer and tribal heritage. The elegant furnishings reveal such subtle touches as peaches carved into a cherrywood console on the second floor landing—a reminder of Jacob Hamblin, a church missionary to the Hopi in Arizona who is known for planting peach trees. Artwork depicting scenes from the Book of Mormon and the Bible hangs throughout the temple.

Solid cherrywood accented with gold leaf trims the interior. Beehives, a symbol of industry in the church, decorate the heavy, brass door handles. Temples typically do not contain stained glass, but a church member found and donated an antique window depicting Jesus and children.

Location: Snowflake.
Description: The 108th Mormon temple built in the world.
How to get there: Follow AZ 277 east into Snowflake. (If you get to AZ 77, where AZ 277 ends, you have gone too far; from AZ 77, you can see the temple on the hill.) After Hillcrest Drive, take the first right turn (south) onto Frontier Parkway. After a short distance, go right (west) on Canyon Drive, which ends in the temple parking lot.

In the ordinance room, where the first instructions and teachings are given, a mural depicting Arizona landscapes covers the walls. In the celestial room, the temple's highest point both physically and spiritually, the furniture is white, gold, and light blue. The room represents the presence of God and the reward of the afterlife.

LDS church members actively trace family genealogies. They perform ordinances in the name of deceased ancestors so that those who passed away without receiving the church's message will have the chance to embrace Christ and to forever join with their families.

Most church activities take place in meetinghouses, but the most important rites occur in the temple. As a symbol of purity and of equality before God, members of the church wear only white clothing when visiting the temple. At the temple, the "House of the Lord," members learn church teachings and religious ceremonies are performed for the living and the deceased. The authority of the holy priesthood seals marriages and families so they may exist together throughout eternity. As a central tenet of the church, baptisms by full immersion also occur in temples.

Prophet Joseph Smith founded the Church of Jesus Christ of Latter-day Saints in 1830 as the restoration of Jesus' church on Earth. According to church teachings, he found and translated the church's sacred record of Jesus' ministry in North and South America, inscribed on gold plates found in New York. LDS church members consider this translation, called the Book of Mormon, to be Scripture along with the Bible.

91. The Church of the Open Bible Lutheran Apache Mission

AZ 73 and Oak Street
Whiteriver, AZ 85941
(928) 338-4069
E-mail: openbible@wmonline.com

Mailing address:
P.O. Box 519
Whiteriver, AZ 85941

The Church of the Open Bible Lutheran Apache Mission is the oldest and largest church in Whiteriver. The white clapboard church topped by a simple cross stands as the legacy of a missionary and son who worked with the White Mountain Apache Tribe. E.E. Guenther arrived from Wisconsin in 1910, when Arizona was still a territory. The missionary won the respect of the Apache people at a time when they

Location: Whiteriver.

Description: A historic church on the Fort Apache Indian Reservation where the next to the last Apache chief was baptized.

How to get there: The church is on the corner of AZ 73 and Oak Street. It's 2 miles past the city limits sign when you're traveling north from AZ 73.

had little reason to trust a white man. Although Guenther respected the native religion, he did not accept tenets contrary to the Bible.

The church was founded in 1912, seven years before a terrible flu epidemic struck. Guenther and his wife, Minnie, nursed many people back to health, including Chief Alchesay, the next to the last chief of the Apache (they now have a tribal chairman) and recipient of the Congressional Medal of Honor. On the day of the church building's dedication in 1922, Chief Alchesay was baptized there along with 100 others. When the chief died, he was buried with the church key in his hand—the same key he used to unlock the door at the church's dedication. As death approached him, the chief said of the key, "This is the key that opened God's house for me and my people, and this is the key that opened heaven for me."

E.E. and Minnie Guenther named their sixth child after the chief, who held Alchesay Arthur Guenther as he was baptized and called him his godson. A.A. Guenther succeeded his father as pastor of the church. Together, they served nearly nine decades in the same pulpit, their lives intertwining with those of the people.

The Rev. A.A. Guenther, a volunteer firefighter, started Little League baseball on the reservation. He speaks Apache and helped the community develop a library to restore the written Apache history. He recently retired at 78 years old, and the Rev. Daniel Rautenberg now leads the congregation.

The church is part of the Wisconsin Evangelical Lutheran Synod. Sunday services commence at 9:30 a.m.

Retreats

92. St. Anthony's Monastery

4784 N. St. Joseph's Way
Florence, AZ 85232
(928) 868-3188
E-mail: monastery@stanthonysmonastery.org
www.stanthonysmonastery.org

The Orthodox Christian monks did not choose the property now home to St. Anthony's Monastery—it chose them. When the fathers showed up with a real estate agent at the 106-acre parcel south of Florence, they heard bells ringing from the empty desert. They took it as a sign that God had brought them to the right place to create a sanctuary of peace and purpose.

That was in 1995. Today, two churches, four chapels, and guest houses are among the buildings at the monastery. The monks are starting to plant an olive grove and are planning other buildings as the community grows.

St. Anthony, born in the third century, denied everything to follow Christ. The modern monks do the same, praying and working together in the way of the early Christian church. Even in the Arizona desert, the monks wear traditional long, black robes. Solitude, prayer, fasting, exercise, work, and obedience mark the community's life as it preserves the traditions of the church.

Location: South of Florence.

Description: A Greek Orthodox monastery open for one- to 10-day stays.

How to get there: From AZ 79, go east on Paisano Drive between mileposts 124 and 125. This will be 8 miles south of Florence. Follow Paisano Drive and go left when it dead-ends at unmarked St. Joseph's Way, which leads to the monastery's parking lot.

For more than 1,000 years, monasteries have existed at Holy Mount Athos in Greece, and Christians have sought blessings and guidance from such communities. In recent years, the Greek Orthodox Church has begun to establish monasteries in North America, noting that Christians here need the same examples of Christian life and devotion to God. In July 1995, five monks from Mount Athos' Holy Monastery of Philotheou began building St. Anthony's, now the largest Greek Orthodox monastery on the continent.

As a way to share the teachings of the Orthodox Christian Church with a world searching for peace, St. Anthony's also welcomes visitors, from those who are simply curious to the serious retreatant, or pilgrim. With chapels, fountains, and beautiful grounds, the monastery provides a holy place to spend a day or longer in prayer and quiet, a respite from the world spent in God's company.

Walkways wind throughout the property, taking you to a lovely open-air chapel or past the tall bell tower. The churches have no electricity. Inside, icons and carvings tell the stories of the faith, and beeswax candles and incense scent the air. Along the walls, seats open to create kneeling benches for prayer. During services, you are expected to stand.

Visitors must stop at the bookstore upon arrival. Please respect these holy grounds by dressing modestly. Everyone should wear socks, even with sandals. Men should wear long pants and long-sleeved shirts. Women should wear long skirts that go well below the knees, long-sleeved blouses, and scarves covering their hair; they should avoid wearing sheer stockings and skirts with slits. The bookstore has a limited supply of scarves, but visitors should be prepared and come dressed appropriately.

Smoking is strictly forbidden, and parents should closely supervise children at all times. Loud talking and laughing are out of place within the serenity of the grounds. You may take photographs of the grounds, the buildings, and church interiors (except during services), but ask permission before photographing any of the monks or the guests.

The best hours to visit the monastery are between 10 a.m. and 4:15 p.m. daily. A monk leads tours and answers questions about Orthodoxy. With advance permission, day visitors are free to attend daily services. The Midnight Hour, Orthros, and Divine Liturgy take place between 3:30 a.m. and 7 a.m. The Ninth Hour and Vespers are from 5 p.m. to 6:15 p.m., and the Small Compline is from 6:45 p.m. to 7:15 p.m. Times of services may change with the celebration of Feast Days.

Only Orthodox Christians may enter the main area of the church during services, according to the Holy Canons of the Orthodox Church. All others may participate from the narthex, the first room upon entering the church. During services, men stand on the right and women on the left. Holy Communion is limited to Orthodox Christians who have prepared with confession and have permission from their spiritual father.

In the dining hall, called the Trapeza, only the monks, Orthodox Christians, and Catechumens (those studying the faith) may be seated during a formal meal. After the meal has ended, guests have a blessing to come in and eat. The monks do not charge for meals or to stay at the retreat houses, but a donation is customary. Orthodox Christians believe that supporting the monks is a virtue and a blessing.

Pilgrims may stay from one to 10 days. Reservations must be made in advance and longer stays can be specially arranged. Men and women stay in separate guest houses and they are not allowed to enter the guest house of the opposite sex. Each guest house has rooms with multiple twin beds and a common kitchen and living room. Pilgrims staying on the property are expected to attend all the scheduled services and to maintain the quiet hours, from 8 p.m. to 3 a.m. and during the three hours following the morning service.

Most pilgrims are Orthodox, but a few non-Orthodox retreatants— especially those interested in becoming Orthodox—stay here. They are drawn to this spiritual and peaceful place where seven or more hours of the day are simply spent in prayer.

On November 10, 1997, His Holiness Ecumenical Patriarch Bartholomew —the world's leader of the Greek Orthodox Church—visited St. Anthony's on the only Arizona stop he made during his U.S. tour. Among Orthodox Christians, he is considered the first among equals and the 270th successor to the Apostle Andrew. The Orthodox Church does not teach the infallibility of its leader, as does the Roman Catholic Church.

The Greek Orthodox Church is one of the four historic patriarchates that remain in communion from the time of Jesus. The church was unified until A.D. 1054, when the Roman Patriarch broke away to form the Roman Catholic Church. Today, more than 300 million Orthodox Christians live throughout the world.

93. Essence of Tranquility

6074 Lebanon Loop Rd.
Safford, AZ 85546
(928) 428-9312
(877) 895-6810
E-mail: tranquil@eaznet.com
www.members.tripod.com/azhotspring

At Essence of Tranquility, embraced by the warm waters of Mother Earth, you feel the spirit flow. Good energy and happiness fill the air, as you relax and let go of the cares of daily life.

The hot spring's water comes from an artesian flow well that was drilled in 1949, and it is not pumped, heated, or cooled. The mineral water, which is high in sodium and feels silky, comes out of the ground at 108 degrees. Temperatures in the six concrete soaking tubs range from 98 degrees to 106 degrees. The five private tubs measure 4 or more feet deep and each has a theme. The most soothing area for a soak has a rock waterfall and a pool deep enough for floating.

You can tent-camp overnight for $10 per person or sleep in teepees near the medicine wheel. The small teepee costs $20 a night for one person. The medium-size, 14-foot teepee is $30 for one or two people. The largest

Location: South of Safford.

Description: A natural hot spring for soaking, with overnight stays in teepees.

How to get there: From milepost 115 on US 191, go west on Cactus Road. Drive 0.5 mile and turn right (north) on Lebanon Loop Road. Essence of Tranquility is about 0.25 mile on the left.

teepee, which sleeps up to nine people, is $80 a night. A small trailer with two twin beds can be rented for $45 a night. Reservations are required for overnight stays. For soaking, reservations are accepted, but people often just stop by.

Clarisse Drake bought the property in 1993 and turned the longtime bathhouse into a place of calm to reconnect spiritually and heal physically. Therapeutic treatments, massage, energy work, and herbal detox wraps are available. Painted clouds decorate the walls of the soothing treatment room. The place has become popular for women's retreats and meditation groups, and a good spirit watches over the place and its guests, Drake says.

Alcohol, drugs, and open nudity are not permitted. Clothing is optional in the five private soaking areas, but in the communal tub, clothing is required. Soap, shampoo, and shaving cream are prohibited in the soaking tubs.

Prices for soaking start at $5 per person for up to an hour or $10 per person for day use. Soaking is included with teepee rental or the camping fee. Soaking hours are 2 p.m. to 9 p.m. Monday, 8 a.m. to 9 p.m. Tuesday through Saturday, and 8 a.m. to 7 p.m. Sunday.

Sacred Places

94. Mogollon Rim

Rim Country Regional Chamber of Commerce

100 W. Main St. **Mailing address:**

Payson, AZ 85547 P.O. Box 1380

(928) 474-4515 Payson, AZ 85547

(800) 672-9766

E-mail: rcrc@rimcountrychamber.com

www.rimcountrychamber.com

Pinetop-Lakeside Chamber of Commerce

P.O. Box 4220

Pinetop, AZ 85935

(928) 367-4290

(800) 573-4031

E-mail: info@pinetoplakesidechamber.com

www.pinetoplakesidechamber.com

Location: Eastern Arizona.

Description: The edge of the Colorado Plateau, where Arizona's landscape changes dramatically.

How to get there: AZ 260 from Payson to Heber is one of the most scenic driving routes through Rim Country.

*W*here the desert meets millions of acres of pine trees in high-mountain country, the Mogollon Rim splits Arizona into two distinct landscapes. From Payson, the southern edge of the Colorado Plateau stretches across national forests and Indian reservations, beyond eastern Arizona's borders and into New Mexico.

Those in the Wiccan and broader pagan community have a special affinity for the forests on the Rim as places of good energy. Within the Apache-Sitgreaves National Forest is Mt. Baldy, a site sacred to the Apache. The White Mountain Apache Tribe does not grant public access to the top of the mountain.

Multiple campgrounds and hiking trails cover the Mogollon Rim, too many to list here. And, depending on the season and fire restrictions, different trails are open at different times. To find out what's accessible and how to make campground reservations, start by contacting the Chamber of Commerce at Pinetop-Lakeside. Also read *Arizona's Mogollon Rim, Travel Guide to Payson and Beyond* by Don Dedera, published by Arizona Highways Books. And, if you're visiting and prefer to blend in with the locals, Mogollon is pronounced "Muggy-OWN."

95. Petrified Forest National Park

P.O. Box 2217
Petrified Forest National Park, AZ 86028
(928) 524-6228
E-mail: PEFO_Superintendent@nps.gov
www.nps.gov/pefo

The colorful Painted Desert is a geological landscape extending from the Holbrook area to the eastern edge of the Grand Canyon. The Petrified Forest, within the Painted Desert, is known across the globe for its beauty and for its status as one of the world's largest concentrations of petrified wood. The wood fragments scattered throughout Petrified Forest National Park date to the Triassic Period, 250 to 200 million years ago. Also within this 93,500-acre park are signs of more recent human history—petroglyphs and a 100-room pueblo—dating to about 750 years ago.

The drive through the park, which has three visitors' centers along the way, is 28 miles. You can enter the park from either the north or the south. A park pass, valid for a week, is $10 for a private vehicle and $5 for bicyclists and walk-ins. The park is open from 8 a.m. to 5 p.m. (Mountain Standard Time) every day except Christmas Day. Hours extend to 7 a.m. to 7 p.m. in the summer. Overnight camping is not permitted but, with a free permit (available at the visitors' centers on the north and south ends of the park), overnight backpacking is allowed in the Petrified Forest Wilderness.

The park, designated a national monument in 1906 and a national park in 1962, currently has an average of 50,000 visitors per month. Even with the high volume of people here, in such a large park it's easy to find time alone to contemplate the wonders of nature. Many people simply drive through rather than stopping to look at the petroglyphs or the pueblo.

Location: East of Holbrook.

Description: One of the world's largest concentrations of petrified wood and a site of ancestral Native American pueblos and petroglyphs.

How to get there: The south park entrance is 25 miles east of Holbrook. If you are going east on I-40, take Exit 285 or 286 for Holbrook, then go southeast for 19 miles on US 180 and follow the signs to the park's south entrance. The 28-mile loop through the park takes you through the Petrified Forest in the Painted Desert, and you will meet up with I-40 at Exit 311. If you are going west on I-40, you can take Exit 311 into the park and start at the loop's north end.

At the Puerco Pueblo archaeological site, a 0.5-mile paved trail takes you by the pueblo, a kiva, and several overlooks to view petroglyphs. Each year at the summer solstice, you may observe a dagger of light piercing the center of a circular petroglyph, marking the longest day of the year. To help park visitors observe this phenomenon, rangers present programs for a two-week period in June. South of Puerco Pueblo, Newspaper Rock is another petroglyph site worth seeing.

Starting from the Rainbow Forest Museum at the park's south entrance, the paved Agate House Trail is about 1 mile roundtrip. The path leads to a structure that was built from petrified wood and adobe by the Ancestral Puebloans.

The area was made a national park to preserve its large concentration of petrified wood. The wood's brilliant colors, created by mineral deposits, make it tempting for visitors to want to take some home with them. Visitors steal an estimated ton of petrified wood per month, according to the park. Many people over the years have anonymously returned the rocks with letters of apology. Some have attributed bad luck to stealing a rock. Federal law prohibits removing from the park any petrified wood, or other archaeological item, and violators could be fined, imprisoned, or both. Taking even the smallest piece of petrified wood could result in a minimum fine of $275. Please avoid the temptation and purchase your piece of petrified wood in gift shops, which get their wood not from the park but on private land outside park boundaries.

The visitors' centers have more detailed information and maps. At the north entrance is the Painted Desert Visitor Center, which screens a 20-minute video about the park every 30 minutes. Several miles into the park, another visitors' center called the Painted Desert Inn overlooks the desert of the same name. The Rainbow Forest Museum at the south entrance of the park has exhibits on geology and paleontology, including casts of early Triassic dinosaurs.

96. Besh-Ba-Gowah Archaeological Park

Jesse Hayes Road
Globe, AZ 85501
(928) 425-0320

Mailing address:
150 N. Pine St.
Globe, AZ 85501

*M*odern visitors enter the ancestral pueblo at Besh-Ba-Gowah the same and only way its ancient inhabitants did: through a long corridor, past storage rooms, fire pits, and small doorways. Likely, the Salado people who lived here covered the corridor more than 700 years ago for purposes of defense.

Besh-Ba-Gowah, a name given by the Apache, means "metal camp." The site once was home to a 200-room, multilevel pueblo that housed about 360 people at its peak. The Salado began construction here around A.D. 1225 and abandoned the site around 1400. These ancient people might have migrated to Zuni regions or traveled south into Mexico. Artifacts left behind such as copper bells from central Mexico and shells from the Gulf of Mexico indicate that the Salado traded extensively, but little is known about them. Although they interacted with the Hohokam,

Location: Globe.

Description: An ancestral pueblo built by the ancient Salado people.

How to get there: From US 60 in Globe, follow the signs to the park. They will take you north on Oak Street for two blocks. Go right (east) on Broad Street for 0.5 mile, then right (southeast) on Jesse Hayes Road. Turn right (south) before Ice House Canyon Bridge and continue into the park. Go through the first parking lot to the one at the visitors' center.

who lived in a pit-house settlement in the area from about A.D. 900 to 1100, the Salado maintained a distinct lifestyle.

Parts of the pueblo have been reconstructed using the most likely original construction technique, based on archaeological evidence and theory. You get a sense of how a family would have lived—in a room smaller than a one-car garage.

One room, though, is different, and archaeologists speculate the Salado might have used it for ceremonies and ritual. It's the only such room discovered at a large Salado site. The Salado would have entered through the roof into the room, which had benches made of earth along three sides. An altar might have existed on the east side. Below the altar is a small, square hole that archaeologists believe might be a sipapu, an "earth navel where spirits can pass from middle earth to this world," as a sign explains. The sipapu was once filled with ground turquoise and sealed by a large quartz crystal.

The museum contains fine examples of pottery, turquoise and shell jewelry, and fragments of cotton cloth. Your visit begins with a short movie describing the vanished culture. The masonry pueblo's rocks would not have been exposed, but covered with a smooth clay and mud plaster, according to a reconstruction in the visitors' center.

The park is open from 9 a.m. to 5 p.m. daily. Admission is $3 for adults, $2 for seniors, and free for children 12 and under. The site has picnic tables and a shady park with playground equipment; more picnic areas are nearby.

97. Casa Malpais Archaeological Park

318 E. Main St.
Springerville, AZ 85938
(928) 333-5375
E-mail: malpais@cybertrails.com
www.casamalpais.com

Mailing address:
P.O. Box 870
Springerville, AZ 85938

Casa Malpais, an ancestral sacred site for the Hopi and Zuni, features extensive petroglyphs that mark solstices and equinoxes, as well as a Great Kiva with walls 3 feet thick and 8½ feet tall. Different from the round kivas built by the Anasazi, this Great Kiva of the Mogollon people is square. Religious ceremonies were held at kivas—the places where ancient people went when they needed rain or healing, or when they were ready to plant or harvest crops.

About two years ago, Zuni and Hopi tribal members had performed a ceremonial dance in the plaza to give blessings back to Mother Earth and its inhabitants. Two red-tailed hawks, two eagles, and a deer made their presence known during the ceremony. And although it hadn't rained in ages, it soon poured.

Location: Springerville.

Description: An extensive archaeological site featuring a Great Kiva.

How to get there: Springerville is on US 60, about 25 miles west of the Arizona–New Mexico border. US 60 turns into Main Street through Springerville. The visitors' center and museum are clearly marked with a sign.

Casa Malpais site manager Vicki J. Goin has often felt the energy of the place, as have visitors. Sometimes in the Great Kiva, the hair on the back of your neck stands up and you get chills, she says, but it's a good feeling. One woman told Goin that she had lived there in another life, which is why she felt such a connection to the place. But for most people, the overwhelming sense here is one of peace. Although the highway is visible from the site, it's as if the signs and stresses of modern life disappear.

Approximately between A.D. 1250 and 1450, the Mogollon inhabited the 17-acre site that overlooks the Round Valley, where they farmed. No one knows for sure why the Mogollon left the area, but theories run the gamut. Once, a tour group fresh from Roswell, New Mexico, was convinced that one petroglyph represented an alien calling up to the mothership, suggesting that perhaps the Mogollon's disappearance from the area had UFO connections. Goin is not so sure. She thinks the migration had more to do with a scarcity of water in the area.

She does know that the ancient ones were ingenious. They built a hidden staircase from the Round Valley floor up the 500-foot cliff, possibly for purposes of defense. Sometimes the screams of eagles echo as you climb the staircase.

The walls of the Great Kiva are made of dry-laid basalt, meaning they were constructed without mortar. The timbers for the roof came from at least 10 miles away, and the foundation stones for the roof's supports are still visible on the floor. A bench made of stone follows the inside wall. A stone wall, possibly an altar or a structure to deflect the wind, stands just inside the entrance.

With 60 rooms, the first floor of the pueblo resembled an apartment block. Parts of the pueblo had second and third stories for a total of about 120 rooms. The pueblo probably housed between 200 and 400 people.

The site is also home to unusual catacomb burial sites, an astronomical observatory, astronomically aligned shrines, and many solar petroglyph markers. Archaeologists speculate this eclectic combination of features means this site might have drawn people from other pueblos for ceremonies and perhaps a regional marketplace.

The astronomical observatory is an oval wall of stone about 3 feet high, with five openings. Four of the openings align with the sun's position at the equinoxes, the solstices, or both. The fifth opening aligns with the north.

Petroglyphs found on the site appear to indicate the times of planting. At sunset on May 5, the sun hits half of a spiral petroglyph, bisecting it into shadow and sunlight. May 5 marks the spring crossquarter, the day halfway between the equinox and solstice. Precisely 24 hours later, the sun hits the first mark inside the spiral. The Mogollon might have taken this as a sign to move down to the valley's floor and start planting. Next to the spiral petroglyph is one of a humanoid foot and another of a shaman with his hands up, likely indicating a blessing or prayer for the crops.

Basque sheepherders gave Casa Malpais its name, which means "House of the Badlands." The site is near the Springerville Volcanic Field, the third largest volcanic field in the continental United States.

To view Casa Malpais, you must meet a guide at the visitors' center and museum, then drive about 1 mile to the site. Tour times typically are 8 a.m. to 4 p.m. daily during the winter. Summer hours are 7 a.m. to 5 p.m. Monday through Friday, and 8 a.m. to 5 p.m. Saturday and Sunday. Call ahead to check on tour times because they can change. The cost is $5 per adult; $4 for seniors, students ages 12 to 18, and college students with identification; and $3 for children under 12. The museum displays Mogollon artifacts and the store sells pottery, kachinas, and other items.

The moderate hike is about 1 mile long, and the tour takes 1½ hours. At 7,000 feet in elevation, summer days here are cooler than elsewhere in the state, but they can still be sunny and hot. Be prepared by bringing water, bug repellant, and sunscreen, and wearing hiking boots.

98. Roadside Shrine on US 60

US 60, just southwest of Miami

As you head east on this dark and winding stretch of US 60, around the last curve before you reach Miami, candles constantly glow from a roadside shrine—a reminder of the continuous prayers of the people who stop here.

Location: Near Miami.
Description: A small roadside grotto with benches for prayer.
How to get there: From US 60 in Miami, the shrine is southwest of town, just past milepost 242.

Built by a Korean War veteran in 1977 to fulfill his promise to the Virgin Mary, the grotto commemorates those who died in the mines of Miami and Globe. A statue of the Virgin Mary is most prominent in the round grotto with benches and bushes. All around her, candles burn.

Through the years, those both familiar with the shrine and those just passing by have left behind photographs, mementos, and newspaper clippings along with their prayers. A clipping of a story about a grandmother and baby who died in a fire was prominently displayed one day. The grandmother perished trying to save her granddaughter. A handwritten note repeats a quote in the story: "I told my mom, 'Don't be sad. Grandma will now take care of Jackie in heaven.'"

The experience is at once sobering and uplifting. So many people have poured out their sorrows here, and yet they have also shared joys. Prayers have been said for the victims of the September 11 attacks, and thanks have been given for the survivors.

The shrine has a wide parking area so you can pull well off US 60, a busy stretch of highway. Somehow, though, when lost in prayer, you no longer notice the cars and trucks whizzing by.

99. Kinishba Ruins

White Mountain Apache Cultural Center and Museum
P.O. Box 507
Fort Apache, AZ 85926
(928) 338-4625
www.wmat.nsn.us/wmaculture.shtml

Kinishba Ruins is an ancestral pueblo on a remote part of the Fort Apache Indian Reservation. Because of its location and lack of an on-site visitors' center, you are asked first to visit the White Mountain Apache Cultural Center and Museum for information on admission to the site.

The center and museum provide non-Apache people with an opportunity to understand the history, complexity, and vitality of White Mountain Apache culture through exhibits and educational programs. It also serves the local White Mountain Apache community by hosting meetings, an artist-in-residence program, and acting as a repository for items of cultural importance.

Location: Near Whiteriver.

Description: An ancestral pueblo near the White Mountain Apache Cultural Center and Museum.

How to get there: Take AZ 73 south from Whiteriver about 4 miles. Go left (east) on Indian Route 46. Follow the signs to the historic park and museum.

The center and museum are part of Fort Apache Historic Park. Fort Apache served as an Army outpost from 1870 to 1922, and the oldest surviving building dates to 1871. Other historic structures include the Theodore Roosevelt Indian Boarding School, started in 1923 by the Bureau of Indian Affairs after the Army left.

The cultural center and the museum are open from 8 a.m. to 5 p.m. Monday through Friday, and during the same hours on summer Saturdays. Admission is $3 for adults and $2 for students and seniors. Children under 10 are admitted free of charge.

From the cultural center, you will be given directions to Kinishba Ruins, located a few miles away on a well-maintained dirt road. Save for the sounds of the wind and birds, an intense quiet rules Kinishba. The site has no interpretation, but a sign does remind you of its sacred nature: "This area is sacred to the Apache and is a precious and irreplaceable part of our national heritage....Apache tradition forbids the disturbance of sacred areas." Federal law does, too, so look but do not touch.

The stone walls were excavated in the 1930s by archaeologist Byron Cummings, who rebuilt some of them during eight years of excavation. The standing walls are his interpretation of how the structure might have looked. Some of the rebuilt walls have crumbled again, while others stand tall in the sprawling pueblo. Funding for the project ended with the advent of World War II, so the other pueblos in the area remain unexcavated.

The large pueblo was occupied from A.D. 1250 to around 1400 by the Ancestral Puebloan People, with whom the Hopi and Zuni share an ancestral and cultural affinity. Clan migration stories connect the Ancestral Puebloan People to the area, and the Hopi and Zuni have interacted and traded with the White Mountain Apache for centuries.

100. Mt. Graham

Graham County Chamber of Commerce
1111 Thatcher Blvd.
Safford, AZ 85546
(928) 428-2511
(888) 837-1841
E-mail: director@graham-chamber.com
www.graham-chamber.com

$\mathcal{M}$t. Graham, a scenic focus in Safford and the surrounding area, rises to more than 10,000 feet in the Pinaleno Mountains. Some Safford residents say they can feel a positive energy coming down from the mountain and good spirits watching over them.

The San Carlos Apache hold sacred this lofty peak, believing

Location: Southwest of Safford.

Description: A beautiful mountain that is sacred to the San Carlos Apache Tribe.

How to get there: In Safford, US 70 turns into Thatcher Boulevard. The chamber of commerce is on Thatcher Boulevard between 20th and Eighth avenues.

that spirits dwell here and that the mountain takes prayers to heaven. Located in Coronado National Forest with campgrounds and picnic areas nearby, the mountain also houses the Mt. Graham International Observatory. The San Carlos Apache opposed the project on the grounds that it would destroy the sacredness of the mountain where some of their ceremonies take place, but they lost in court.

Contact the Graham County Chamber of Commerce before you plan your trip, as the forests and parks sometimes close because of fire danger or budget cuts. Tours of the mountain and of the telescopes depart from the chamber or the observatory. These forays start at $20 per person and include lunch.

If you prefer a self-guided excursion, you can drive up Swift Trail Road, a paved, curvy, 35-mile road to the top of the mountain. From US 70, take US 191 south to Swift Trail Road. Occasionally, the road closes because of snow, which is relatively rare in the Safford area.

When it's open, Roper Lake State Park at the base of Mt. Graham is a good place for spending the day or for overnight camping. The park has fishing opportunities and a natural hot spring. It's located at 101 E. Roper Lake Rd., 6 miles south of Safford off US 191. Day use hours are 6 a.m. to 10 p.m., and park entry and camping fees vary.

Appendix
Arizona Religious and Tribal Organizations

Although some of the following organizations appear as full entries in the book, this appendix mainly includes supplemental information to get you connected with various denominations, statewide religious groups, and local tribes. You can reference this list to locate the nearest house of worship, find out about cultural activities at Native American sites, and more.

African Methodist Episcopal Church
Prince Chapel A.M.E. Church, Tucson, (520) 624-2871
Tanner Chapel A.M.E., Phoenix, (602) 253-8426

Assemblies of God
Assemblies of God Arizona District Council, Phoenix, (602) 252-5515

Bahá'í Faith
Bahá'í Faith Information Center, Phoenix, (602) 861-1609

Baptist
American Baptist Churches of Arizona, Glendale, (623) 846-8823
Arizona Southern Baptist Convention, Phoenix, (480) 945-0880,
    (800) 687-2431
National Baptist Convention of America, First Institutional Baptist Church,
    Phoenix, (602) 258-1998
Southwest Conservative Baptist Association, Phoenix, (602) 788-8090

Buddhist
Arizona Buddhist Temple, Phoenix, (602) 278-0036
Bodhi Heart Group at St. Stephen's Episcopal Church, Phoenix,
    (602) 840-0437
Bodhisattva Institute, Tucson, (520) 325-2272
Center for Buddhist Development, Tempe, (480) 777-1434
Garchen Buddhist Institute, Chino Valley, (928) 925-5847
Haku-un-ji Zen Center, Tempe, (480) 894-6353
Tucson Community Meditation Center, (520) 869-6511

Christian Science
First Church of Christ, Scientist, Tucson, (520) 325-1181
Second Church of Christ, Scientist, Phoenix, (602) 265-9445

Church of Jesus Christ of Latter-day Saints

Church of Jesus Christ of Latter-day Saints Visitors' Center, Mesa, (480) 964-7164

Episcopalian

Episcopal Diocese of Arizona, Phoenix, (602) 254-0976

Evangelical Lutheran Church in America

Evangelical Lutheran Church in America, Grand Canyon Synod, Phoenix, (602) 957-3223

Lutheran Social Ministry of the Southwest, Mesa, (480) 654-4539

Greek Orthodox

Holy Trinity Greek Orthodox Cathedral, Phoenix, (602) 264-7863

Hindu

International Society for Krishna Consciousness Temple, Chandler, (480) 705-4900

Maha Ganapati Temple of Arizona, Maricopa, (480) 644-1252

Islamic

Islamic Center of Tucson, (520) 624-3233

Islamic Cultural Center of Tempe, (480) 894-6070

Jewish

American Jewish Committee, Scottsdale, (480) 970-6363

Jewish Federation of Greater Phoenix, Scottsdale, (480) 634-4900

Jewish Federation of Southern Arizona, Tucson, (520) 577-9393

Native American

Inter Tribal Council of Arizona, Phoenix, (602) 258-4822

Region 1, Phoenix and Vicinity
Fort McDowell Yavapai Nation, Fountain Hills, (480) 837-5121
Salt River Pima-Maricopa Indian Community, Scottsdale, (480) 850-8056

Region 2, Tucson and Southern Arizona
Ak-Chin Indian Community, Maricopa, (520) 568-2227
Cocopah Tribe, Somerton, (928) 627-2061
Fort Yuma-Quechan Tribe, Yuma, (760) 572-0661
Gila River Indian Center (Arts and Crafts Center), Sacaton, (520) 315-3411
Pascua Yaqui Tribe, Tucson, (520) 883-5000
Tohono O'odham Nation, Sells, (520) 383-2028

Region 3, Prescott and West-Central Arizona
Yavapai-Apache Nation, Camp Verde, (928) 567-3649
Yavapai-Prescott Indian Tribe, Prescott, (928) 445-8790

Native American (continued)
Region 4, Grand Canyon and Northern Arizona
Colorado River Indian Tribes, Parker, (928) 669-9211
Fort Mohave Indian Tribe, Needles, Calif., (760) 629-4591
Havasupai Tribe, Supai, (928) 448-2121
Hopi Tribe, Kykotsmovi, (928) 734-3000
Hualapai Tribe, Peach Springs, (928) 769-2234
Kaibab-Paiute Tribe, Fredonia, (928) 643-7245
Navajo Nation, Window Rock, (928) 871-6436
San Juan Southern Paiute Tribe, Tuba City, (928) 283-4587

Region 6, East-Central Arizona
San Carlos Apache Tribe, San Carlos, (928) 475-2361
Tonto Apache Tribe, Payson, (928) 474-6044, (800) 777-7529, ext. 158
   (Mazatzal Casino)
White Mountain Apache Tribe, Fort Apache, (928) 338-4625

New Age
New Age Community Church, Phoenix, (602) 237-3213

Pagan/Wiccan/Metaphysical
Magickal Paths, Tempe, (480) 237-4000

Presbyterian (USA)
Presbytery of Grand Canyon, Phoenix, (602) 468-3820, (800) 557-3820

Roman Catholic
Catholic Social Service, Phoenix, (602) 285-1999
Roman Catholic Diocese of Phoenix, (602) 257-0030
Roman Catholic Diocese of Tucson, (520) 792-3410

Seventh-day Adventist
Arizona Conference of the Seventh-day Adventists, Scottsdale,
   (480) 991-6777

Unitarian Universalist
Unitarian Universalist Congregation of Phoenix, (602) 840-8400

United Methodist
United Methodist Church Desert Southwest Annual Conference, Phoenix,
   (602) 266-6956, (800) 229-8622

Other Organizations
Arizona Interfaith Movement, Phoenix, (602) 277-2484
Arizona Ecumenical Council, Phoenix, (602) 468-3818
Christian Business Women's Association, Phoenix, (480) 948-2292
Christian Motorsports International, Gilbert, (480) 507-5323.
The Salvation Army, Phoenix, (602) 267-4100

Index

NOTE: Citations followed by the letter "p" denote photos; citations followed by the letter "m" denote maps.

About the Author/Photographer

elly Ettenborough is a reporter for *The Arizona Republic*, the state's largest newspaper. She has spent most of her reporting career covering religion and spirituality in Arizona, first for the *Mesa Tribune* and then for the *Republic*.

She received awards for her religion stories from the Arizona Press Club

Photo by Trevor Ettenborough

in 1994 and 1996–2002. In 1995, the Religion Newswriters Association named the *Tribune* as runner-up for the best religion section in the United States and Canada. Ettenborough served as president of the Society of Professional Journalists' Valley of the Sun chapter in 1995–1996, and she received the chapter's Workhorse Award for 1994–1995.

She took her first newspaper job during her senior year at East Prairie High School in East Prairie, Mo. In the "Who, What, When, Where and Why" column for the small town's weekly *East Prairie Eagle,* she wrote about dinner parties, the summer's first homegrown tomato, and who caught the biggest catfish. Following her stint at the town paper, she attended the University of Missouri at Columbia and graduated from Arizona State University in 1990.

Ettenborough lives with her husband, Trevor, and their daughter, Ivy, in Peoria, Ariz.